The Treasury of Unearned Gifts

Rebbe Nachman's path to

happiness and contentment in life

by
Chaim Kramer

edited by
Ozer Bergman

Published by
BRESLOV RESEARCH INSTITUTE
Jerusalem/New York

First   edition

For further information:
Breslov Research Institute
POB 5370
Jerusalem, Israel

or:
Breslov Research Institute
POB 587
Monsey, NY 10952-0587

e-mail address: info@breslov.org

This book is dedicated
to the memory of
my grandfather

Mendel Jeret z"l

whose devotion to Judaism
inspired me on my spiritual path

Jay Knopf

Dedicated to G.K.
"A good wife is a genuine gift to her husband" (*Yevamot* 63b).

Many thanks to S.C. Mizrahi and C. Rafael for the criticism I've earned from their treasuries of editing skills.

Table of Contents

The Treasury of Unearned Gifts

Prologue

It was his last summer and he knew it. The fresh air, the spacious gardens, the daily strolls in the city's outskirts, all would soon cease. Having contracted tuberculosis two and a half years earlier, every day of life was treasured as a miracle unto itself.

Rebbe Nachman had just moved to the house in which, two months later, he would breathe his last. As was customary, his followers joined him for Shabbat Nachamu ("Shabbat of Consolation"), which follows the fast of Tish'ah b'Av (the Ninth of Av, the day which marks the destruction of the Holy Temple). Rebbe Nachman was very weak that Friday evening and scarcely had strength to speak. Facing his followers, he said:

> "Why do you come to see me? Don't you realize I know nothing at all now? At this point I am just an ordinary person! The only thing that inspires me is the fact that I have merited being in the Holy Land."

After repeating this theme several times, Rebbe Nachman proceeded to give a most beautiful lesson, expounding upon simplicity, the Holy Land and how

Godliness permeates every facet of existence. Even if someone is unworthy, God is there for him, ready to reveal to him the deepest mysteries of Creation. This is because God has a Treasury of Unearned Gifts that sustains the entire world, even those people who are most distant from Him: there is always hope.

Rebbe Nachman's body was racked with pain, his breathing was laborious and he sometimes coughed up blood. He knew he was dying. Yet this lesson became a powerful source of inspiration even to the Rebbe himself. Out of his pain and suffering, in one of his darkest moments, Rebbe Nachman issued one of the most important messages of all times:

> "*Gevalt!* Never despair! There is never a reason for despair!"

(Rabbi Nachman's Wisdom #153)

* * *

1

"Wouldn't it be nice...?"

Wouldn't it be nice if we all enjoyed the good life: if we all had a limitless repository upon which to draw? Imagine never having to worry about where the money to pay the next grocery bill, mortgage or tuition installment would come from. Think about how nice it would feel to have the freedom to do whatever you wanted, using your own seemingly limitless assets. And wouldn't it be even nicer if we were all blessed with good health — physical, mental and emotional — to help us enjoy that vast treasury?

When speaking about a treasury, most people's first thoughts turn to finances. Nevertheless, many different categories of wealth exist. Good health is one, wisdom is another. A parent or a good friend is a treasure to be cherished.

Our Sages state (*Avot* 4:1), "Who is wealthy? One who is satisfied with his lot." The application of the term "wealthy" to anyone who is satisfied with his or her life is not just a noble ideal. It is a statement of such magnitude that, when clearly understood, opens entirely new vistas on life and can illumine anyone's darkest moments. It is, in fact, the key to a contented life: a life of satisfaction and joy, of emotional stability, of accomplishment and solid relationships — a life in which the daily grind and the challenges can be faced with confidence and security.

Satisfaction is the greatest treasure one can hope for in life, a treasure that exceeds all others. As we shall see, Rebbe Nachman teaches that satisfaction with life is available to all people at all times, and can be had simply by drawing upon the remarkable resources that each person already possesses. Satisfaction is the key to experiencing a tangible sweetness in life, no matter what the circumstances.

*

Each and every person is absolutely unique, each possesses incredible resources. All we need to do is to realize the extent of our inner strength and apply that strength according to our *own* abilities. The reason we are blessed with these resources is that man was created by God: he is dependent upon and attached to Him at all times. We know that God is Infinite. Thus, by extension, the resources upon which we can rely are drawn from a Limitless Source. The more intensely we recognize that Source, the better equipped we are to draw upon it. If we will but cultivate that realization of our Divine connection, we will be able to truly appreciate our selves, and properly utilize our own treasuries.

Each of us, without exception, possesses a vast treasury. "It is mine, all mine; I may do with it as I please." But the irony is that, though it is "mine," it is not really a treasury of my own making. Our lives and the situations with which we are confronted are all God-given: it was He Who planted us from birth within this family, this city, this country, this environment. No one had a choice into which family he would be born and no one had an opportunity, in his early years, to determine his life's progress. All circumstances of birth and subsequent growth and development in early life are not of the individual's choice. It is God Who gave us life, the health we enjoy, the wealth we possess — and the challenges and opportunities we face in life. It is the attitudes we adopt after we mature that determine *how* we live our lives.

As we shall see, this is the theme underlying "The Treasury of Unearned Gifts."

* * *

2

The Treasury of Unearned Gifts

The Bible relates in the account of the golden calf how Moses ascended on High to beg God to forgive the Jews for their sin. After God had granted forgiveness, Moses had a further request: that God reveal to him His glory. God said to him (Exodus 33:19), "I will make all My goodness pass before you… I will be gracious to whom I will be gracious and I will show compassion to whom I will show compassion."

Our Sages teach (*Shemot Rabbah* 45:6) that after Moses had gained forgiveness for the sin of the golden calf, God gave him a "grand tour" of the Heavens and revealed to him the concept of reward and punishment. God also showed him the rewards set aside for the righteous in the World to Come. Moses asked about each treasury, "For whom is this? For whom is that?" God replied, "This one is for those who give charity…that one is for those who raise orphans…."

Moses then saw an immense treasury. He asked, "For whom is this treasury?" God replied, "Those who are deserving, I reward for their numerous good deeds from their own [accumulated treasuries]. But those who lack merit, I reward from this 'Treasury of

Unearned Gifts.' For, 'I will be gracious to whom I will be gracious and I will show compassion to whom I will show compassion'."

This Midrash is puzzling. On the one hand, it instills in us hope that no matter what, even if we succumb to sin, we can still look forward to an ultimate reward. If a person accumulates his own merits, he has "created" his own reward by earning it. If not, although he may have erred or sinned, there is still hope for God's compassion, and thus for some reward from God's Treasury of Unearned Gifts.

On the other hand, the Midrash may seem to indicate that it doesn't matter all that much if a person chooses a life of immorality, idolatry and general sinfulness — since he can always secure a reward from the Treasury of Unearned Gifts. If he has merits, he has his own earned reward. If he sins and is unworthy, well… God says, "I will be gracious to whom I will be gracious and I will show compassion to whom I will show compassion." He'll get a reward anyway, won't he? This parallels, in a sense, the talmudic teaching (Sanhedrin 90a), "All Israel has a portion in the World to Come." That is, every person, whether good or wicked, will eventually receive a portion of Eternal Good in the World to Come.

Somehow this doesn't seem fair. One person strives his entire life to be good, and through this merits reward. He is rewarded according to his deeds; that is to say, his "retirement and pension plan" has accrued as a result of his "investment" in mitzvot. Another person acts frivolously or sinfully, perhaps even wickedly, throughout his life, yet after his passing he can still merit a reward from the limitless resources of God's private treasury! This reward might be compared to a "government handout" — which benefits an entire sector of society, including its most undeserving members. Everyone gets a reward, regardless of his attitude or conduct.

This seems a crude travesty of justice — and yet God is All-Just. There must be some system which determines a person's right to a reward from that Treasury. And there must likewise be some criteria which determine who is worthy to receive a portion from the Treasury of Unearned Gifts and who might be excluded. To help us gain some understanding of this issue, we present Reb Noson's analogy of a "Treasury of Unearned Gifts" from his *magnum opus, Likutey Halakhot,* in the discourse of *Hilkhot Matanah* (4:7).

*

A king decided to reward handsomely each and every one of his subjects, and chose a certain date to celebrate the event. The king wanted all his subjects to join in the festivities, which would also be attended by all his ministers and officials. Out of love and compassion for his subjects, he informed them of his intentions in advance so that they could prepare themselves properly.

They would have to prepare fine clothing, bathe themselves with fine oils, and see that their clothing was adorned with the proper jewels and medals, in order to enter the king's palace and to mingle with his ministers and officers — for only in such a state would a person be worthy of receiving the king's rewards.

The king loved his subjects very much. He understood that not all his subjects would know how to prepare for such a royal celebration and, since anyone who arrived at the festivities dirty in body or garment would certainly not be rewarded, he equipped them with everything they would need. He prepared fine clothing, jewels and accessories, and all types of fine oils and spices. He also advised his subjects that they should properly prepare their garments. In addition, the king sent his royal ministers to the people to teach them everything they would need to know about conduct in the king's palace, such as how to dress with the correct jewels and medals, so that they would not be embarrassed.

Beyond all this, the king and his ministers warned the people to distance themselves from anything which would make them dirty. Out of his love for them, he also ordered his advisors to show the people how to cleanse themselves and their clothing if they became dirty so that they would be fit for a visit to the king's palace. He gave the people fountains and streams where they could cleanse themselves if it became necessary. Even if someone were to become extremely soiled, the streams would be sufficiently effective to cleanse him and his clothing of any impurity. These streams could transform the odor of excrement into the fragrance of sweet-smelling spices.

The king also told them that, as they prepared themselves for the celebration, they could use their finery as they wished and avail themselves of the amenities of the springs and streams. In this way, they would be able to learn to act royally within the king's palace and to fully enjoy the rewards the king intended to bestow upon them — the royal gifts and pleasures that he planned to give freely to his subjects. All this the king did so that his subjects could enjoy his beneficence.

*

God created the world in order to bestow His goodness upon humanity. His advice is contained in the Torah. His ministers are the tzaddikim, who reveal and teach the Word of God. The day of the celebration alludes to the World to Come, when all humanity will be rewarded for their good deeds.

In addition, God provided mankind with everything necessary to prepare for the festivities. Each person has his own lifestyle, determined by his state of health, his upbringing, his education, his livelihood and so on. Each person was placed into unique circumstances and must prepare for the celebration with the tools God granted him. From the time a person begins to mature, having developed according to his circumstances, he is expected to prepare himself, by adorning himself with the garments and spices the King has given him — the "garments and spices" being the good deeds that God has commanded us to perform, which we accomplish through the countless physical, material and emotional blessings He has given us.

Furthermore, man was commanded to keep himself clean from sin, not to soil the "royal garments" (i.e., his possessions, body, mind and soul) that God gave him. However, in case man errs, transgresses or even becomes a sinner, God forbid, the King has prepared remedies for him to cleanse himself and his garments; He has prepared streams and fountains of fine oils and spices that can remove every vestige of sin and spiritual excrement. The remedy God offers is repentance; the streams and fine oils represent Torah, prayer and good deeds.

The time allotted to prepare for the King's celebration is a person's lifetime. During his life he may partake freely of the King's "garments and oils" — that is, Torah and good deeds — and dress himself up in preparation for the festivities. In fact, the King encourages him to do so. The more a person practices the mitzvot of God, the more attuned he becomes to the royal behavior necessary for one who wishes to enter the King's palace and act in accordance with the birthright of nobility. And furthermore, the better equipped that person will be to mingle with God's officers, the tzaddikim.

Those who prepare themselves properly can partake fully of the rewards the King intends to bestow upon them.

*

The analogy is quite basic: God grants life. He also provides each person with the amenities he requires in order to succeed in life. Each person was given a "garment" (body and soul) fitted to his own "measurements," along with the necessary "accessories" — the material requirements that each individual needs to ensure his spiritual development.

But this analogy seems to create a paradox, in that it does not quite correspond to our general understanding of "reward and punishment." We find repeatedly in talmudic literature that the reward that awaits a person is commensurate with his deeds: the more good deeds a person performs the greater will be his reward. If so, the reward of participating in the King's celebration is not taken from a Treasury of Unearned Gifts at all, but rather is based on a person's accomplishments during his lifetime. What, then, is the point of Reb Noson's analogy?

The answer is that in the World to Come each person will indeed be rewarded according to his deeds. Thus, this "Treasury of Unearned Gifts" is something altogether different from the reward of the World to Come, and a simple understanding of its significance can change the course of our lives!

Even a cursory view of our existence will show us that actually all the good deeds we perform are possible only as a result of God's *first* having granted us life and placed us in a position to be able to perform those good deeds. The Treasury of Unearned Gifts consists of God's preliminary gifts to us — the gifts of life, wisdom, strength and property — enabling us to appreciate our abilities and to utilize them as we prepare for the festivities awaiting us in the World to Come.

In its purest sense, the Treasury of Unearned Gifts is life itself, where God's limitless good abounds. If we will but learn to seek this good, we will find it manifest in every facet of our lives. Godliness on this earth is thus the good that is to be found everywhere — though it may be overshadowed by the drudgery of the daily grind of our material existence. If we can but transcend the drudgery and begin to understand that there is a Greater Force Who grants us life in the first place — in order to provide us with the "tools" and "garments" necessary to join in His celebration — then we will begin to see extraordinary "unearned gifts" each day, in every circumstance. To be sure, not every day will hold the most gratifying experiences. In fact, there will undoubtedly be days which will bring with them unbearable suffering. But the awareness that we have gained — that all that happens to us is intended to prepare us for the King's celebration — will enable us to appreciate all the good we do have and to find solace in even the little things in the abundant, continuous "unearned gift" of life itself.

*

In the next chapter, we will review Rebbe Nachman's lesson on the Treasury of Unearned Gifts. Following that, we will present Reb Noson's discourses on how this Treasury may be found in many facets of our lives, so that we may all learn to draw from this Treasury to enrich our lives and to enhance our appreciation of ourselves, our possessions and our relationships. Armed with these understandings, our entire life will take on a new and deeper meaning. It will become a life in which appreciation for everything we have can be truly felt. It will translate into a life of contentment, for everything we experience, whether good or otherwise, is merely another facet of our preparations for the future festivities. The state of our health, our possessions and our various relationships, will help to direct us towards finding gratification in all our endeavors. Our lives will be defined by joy and happiness, by appreciation and spirituality, by lasting relationships and stability — because of the knowledge that we will always be able to find good in our days.

* * *

3

"Va'Etchanan — I pleaded..."

The Jewish calendar is replete with festivals and days of joy, as well as with days of mourning. One period of mourning is "The Three Weeks," which begins on the 17th of Tammuz, the day the wall of Jerusalem was breached nearly 2,000 years ago. On that day the Roman army began its conquest of the Holy City. The Three Weeks culminate on Tish'ah b'Av, the day on which the actual destruction of the Holy Temple, and our exile, began. To commemorate these weeks of calamity, various laws and customs of mourning are enacted and several biblical excerpts of rebuke are read, as a reminder that there is much room for improvement in our lives.

But our Sages teach that suffering is not eternal, that hope is always waiting in the wings. This optimistic approach is built into the Jewish calendar; thus immediately after Tish'ah b'Av begins a seven-week period of consolation. During this time, the famous passages of consolation found in the book of Isaiah are read each week, to comfort the Jews and to encourage them to look forward to a better and brighter future. On the Shabbat following Tish'ah b'Av, the weekly Torah portion is *Va'Etchanan* (Deuteronomy 3:23-7:11). That

Shabbat is also known as Shabbat Nachamu, because the haftarah read that morning is, "*Nachamu! Nachamu! Ami...* — Be consoled! Be consoled! My nation...." (Isaiah 40:1).

It was customary for his followers to gather with Rebbe Nachman for Shabbat Nachamu. Throughout his years as a chassidic master in Breslov, and in his final year in Uman (where he passed away and is interred), Rebbe Nachman's disciples came from far and wide to hear his Torah teachings and to bask in his light on this Shabbat. Following the three weeks of pain and mourning, what could be more meaningful than to recharge one's spiritual batteries with hope — drawn from the very source of Creation, from the Torah itself!

However, in his last year (August 1810), the Rebbe was so ill and weak that his life seemed to mirror more the sufferings of "The Three Weeks" than the harbinger of hope and consolation. When his followers assembled for their yearly gathering, Rebbe Nachman spoke of his fragile condition. Indeed, he was so broken that he said to them, "Why do you come to see me? Don't you realize I know nothing at all now? At this point I am just an ordinary person! The only thing that inspires me is the fact that I have merited being in the Holy Land."

Rebbe Nachman's words may seem at first glance to be a shocking complaint. The Rebbe, despite his terminal illness, was certainly aware of his astounding success, both in achieving great spiritual heights for himself and in preparing the legacy he was to leave behind. Was it pain or melancholy that moved him to make this statement?

In fact, it was neither. When we have studied the entire lesson (beginning on the following page) we will understand that this introductory comment serves as its outline. It alludes to the concepts of connecting to the tzaddik; the need for Torah study; the fact that everybody, even a tzaddik, has ups and downs; the Holy Land and the need to draw upon the Treasury in order to merit being there.

Despite his frail condition, Rebbe Nachman revealed on that Shabbat one of his most awesome and wondrous lessons, which reflects both the theme of the Torah reading of *Va'Etchanan* and the immortal words of Isaiah, *"Nachamu!* Be consoled!"* It is a lesson on the Treasury of Unearned Gifts.

The story behind Rebbe Nachman's revelation of this lesson may be found in *Rabbi Nachman's Wisdom* (#153), and the lesson itself is found in *Likutey Moharan* (II, 78). Following are several excerpts from the lesson, in free translation with commentary. The lesson is quite intricate. In addition to those concepts mentioned above, the Rebbe also discusses: Torah as the source of life; the "ordinary person"; Lovingkindness and the concealed Torah; the path to the Holy Land; simplicity; and never giving up hope. After reviewing the lesson, a brief summary will show how the principles contained within it apply to each and every individual.

*

Likutey Moharan II, 78

"Va'Etchanan — I pleaded to God at that time..."

Deuteronomy 3:23

The term *"Va'Etchanan"* denotes that Moses pleaded with God to give him an unearned gift. Even though the righteous possess many merits of their own, they always plead with God to provide an answer to their prayers from His Treasury of Unearned Gifts.

Rashi, *loc. cit.*

It was the time ordained for Moses' death. Denied entry into the Holy Land, he persisted in pleading and begging that God annul His oath and allow him to enter the Land. Although Moses was a truly righteous man, rather than enumerating his many good deeds and his untiring self-sacrifice for the Jewish Nation, he pleaded with God to grant him an unearned gift from His Treasury. Moses thus opened his prayer with the word *"Va'Etchanan"* — indicating that he was seeking salvation from God's Treasury of Unearned Gifts. Based on this one word, *"Va'Etchanan,"* Rebbe Nachman explains how Moses' plea to enter the Holy Land included all the concepts mentioned above.

Rebbe Nachman taught:

> The verse states (Deuteronomy 30:20), "For it is your life and the length of your days...," telling us that the Torah *is* our very life. Whoever distances himself from Torah distances himself from life (*Zohar* I, 92a).

This idea is rooted in the Midrash which states that, prior to creating the world, God created the Torah. He then used the Torah as a "blueprint" for the creation of the universe and everything in it (*Bereishit Rabbah* 1:1). The Torah thus represents the vitality of life, meaning eternal life; the Torah existed before Creation and continually sustains the world — since all that transpires in this world can be found in some form in its "blueprint." Human life as well, though of relatively short duration, is also sustained by the Torah, as the verse tells us, "it is your life...."

Based on the understanding that the Torah is the essence of life itself, Rebbe Nachman poses the following question:

How can anyone possibly separate himself from Torah for even a moment? Yet it is literally impossible to be attached to Torah continually, day and night, without a second's interruption. Even the most diligent and devoted students of Torah must stop their studies, if only for a few moments, while they tend to their livelihoods and their other physical needs. Nevertheless, Torah is life. Tending to one's material needs is tantamount to rejecting life itself. How can one separate oneself from life even for a second? Furthermore, even if one must distance oneself for a short time, who would choose to abandon Torah if only for a few moments, when in doing so one is knowingly discarding the chance to be attached to life? Since one cannot remain attached to Torah the entire time, from where does a person draw life during that time when he is distant from Torah?

Rebbe Nachman then expands this concept. Man's physical needs are extensive: one must eat, sleep, tend to one's livelihood and the many other material requirements that occupy one's day. While a person — any person — is involved in the mundane occupations of life and is thus unattached to the Torah, he becomes an "ordinary person."

*

The Ordinary Person

The concept of the ordinary person applies to everyone. A person could be a dedicated Torah scholar; he could be a part-time student and work part time; he might work a full day, or in other ways fill his day with anything but Torah; he could be one who denies Torah and he might even be a gentile, of the nations who never received the Torah. No matter who the person is, he must receive his life and life force from the Torah, for "it is your life." Thus, *everybody* lives on account of the Torah.

The problem is that everyone, even the greatest tzaddik and the most dedicated Torah scholar, must interrupt his studies to tend to his material needs. At that moment of interruption he is blocking his connection to life. How much more does this apply to those who have never had the opportunity to study Torah, or to those who don't even want to study it, or even to those who reject it? Aren't these people blocking their connection to life? From where, or from what, do they draw life? Without a connection to Torah, it would seem that they lack any connection to the source of their lives. There must be some type of "interface" by which an ordinary person can always be attached to Torah, even if indirectly, because without Torah a person would be cut off from life itself.

A very great tzaddik, one who is always attached to Torah, serves as this "interface" for all of humanity. This implies that the tzaddik is *always*, on some level, attached to Torah, even when tending to his material needs. When he is involved in his mundane affairs, the tzaddik receives his vitality from the Torah in a concealed form. When he must interrupt his Torah study, he also becomes an "ordinary person," but he remains intrinsically bound up with the Torah in a concealed manner. In this same concealed manner, those who are distant from Torah can also receive their vitality. But as they are distant from Torah to begin with, it is very difficult for them to receive their vitality directly. The tzaddik is attached to Torah, but at the same time he may become an "ordinary person." He therefore acts as a channel: the ordinary people can receive their vitality through him, for he can "interface" both with the Torah and with them. (The reason the tzaddik acts as the "interface" when he is an "ordinary person," rather than when he is attached to the Torah, will become evident as the lesson unfolds.)

*

The Treasury of Unearned Gifts

The Talmud teaches that the world was created for the sake of the Torah. Logically then, the Torah should have been given at the moment the world was created. Yet we find that the Revelation at Sinai did not occur until the time of Moses, twenty-six generations after the world was created. The Torah is life, and yet it was not available to mankind until the twenty-sixth generation. What sustained the world until then? The answer is that in the early generations the world was sustained not by Torah merit, but through the Chesed (Lovingkindness) of God (see *Pesachim* 118a).

Rebbe Nachman continues:

> Know! Every ordinary person — whether he be a Torah scholar who momentarily refrains from Torah study or any other ordinary person — based on the degree to which he is attached to the Torah, receives his vitality from that same lovingkindness of God which sustained the world prior to the Giving of the Torah at Sinai. Receiving one's vitality through that lovingkindness is tantamount to receiving from the Treasury of Unearned Gifts.
>
> For there is indeed a Treasury of Unearned Gifts from which anyone who is lacking merit can receive a gift. But that Treasury is certainly not available to the wicked for, if it were, the very fact of their receiving a gift, notwithstanding their unworthiness, would make them appear more meritorious than the righteous [who had to earn their reward]. Thus the wicked certainly cannot benefit directly from that Treasury. Instead, the Treasury of Unearned Gifts is reserved for the tzaddik — when he becomes an "ordinary person." (And the general populace of ordinary people, including the wicked, receive their vitality from the Treasury of Unearned Gifts, through the tzaddik.)
>
> This concept relates to the spiritual sustenance of the early generations of the world. At that time, the Torah had not yet been given and so people could not have been involved in its fulfillment. Instead, the inhabitants

of the world were engaged in *derekh eretz* (literally "the way of the land," referring to the building of the world, trade and commerce, etc.). Our Sages teach (*Vayikra Rabbah 9:3*), "Great is *derekh eretz*, for it preceded the Torah by twenty-six generations." Interaction between people, accompanied by respect and courtesy, is a manifestation of kindness, comparable to that lovingkindness which God bestowed upon the world during that time when He sustained it even without Torah. That life support was a gift from God, a gift from His Treasury of Unearned Gifts. In the same way, one who is currently distant from Torah receives his vitality from that same source.

Some questions are begging to be answered at this point. Isn't it the Torah that sustains us? If Torah is life and without it one is distant from life, how then, practically speaking, were the early generations sustained? Who drew from the Treasury *then* for all those "ordinary people?" How is the Treasury available to us, the "ordinary people" of *today*? Rebbe Nachman continues:

The world was created with "Ten Sayings" (*Avot 5:1*) which correspond to the Ten Commandments, which in turn include the entire Torah. We find, therefore, that the essence of the Torah was present in the world from its inception, albeit in a concealed form. This concealed Torah corresponds to the Treasury of Unearned Gifts, and it is this that sustained the world prior to the Revelation.

The Talmud points out that the words "And God said" appear nine times in the account of Creation and it is these "sayings" which brought the entire world into being. But our Sages tell us that there were actually "Ten Sayings" with which God created the world. The Talmud resolves this contradiction with the explanation that the word *"Bereishit"* ("In the beginning") is a "concealed saying" (Megilah 21b). That is, although we do not find the words "And God said" before the mention of the initial act of Creation, nevertheless, since all Creation came about through "sayings," *Bereishit* is also reckoned a "saying." Thus the Torah, which corresponds to the Ten Sayings through which Creation took place, did indeed exist in the world from the moment of Creation. But the Torah that was present at that time corresponds to the "concealed saying," hence that Torah is the "concealed Torah"; that is, it was present in every aspect of life, but it was concealed.

We see then that the concealed Torah was found everywhere within the activities of *derekh eretz* that were taking place then — in everyone's work, in all their deeds, in every aspect of their lives — in order to sustain life. This was God's gift to the world from His Treasury of Unearned Gifts; it was the means by which the world was sustained even when people were unable to apply Torah to their own lives.

The same principle is true today as well, although we already have received and possess the Torah. Through the Treasury of Unearned Gifts, which emanates from the lovingkindness of God, a person can receive vitality even though he may be distant from the Source of Life. However, it is only the tzaddik who, even in the most trying of times and circumstances, can remain constantly attached to the Torah. This tzaddik is able to experience Torah even in its concealed form, hidden within *derekh eretz*, in the countless mundane circumstances of life. This is because the tzaddik always prays that God grant him favor from His Treasury of Unearned Gifts. Through his prayers, the tzaddik merits that Treasury, and can experience God's lovingkindness, which sustains life even when one is distant from Torah. Therefore, the more a person attaches himself to the tzaddik (through studying his teachings and following his advice), the greater is the degree of sustenance and life which he can draw, through the tzaddik, from the Treasury of Unearned Gifts.

*

The Holy Land

Rebbe Nachman then explores further the idea of the Treasury of Unearned Gifts as it parallels the concept of the Holy Land: When the tzaddik is on the level of an ordinary person, he draws his vitality from the *derekh eretz* which, Rebbe Nachman explains, is the path (*derekh*) to the *eretz* (land), i.e., the Holy Land.

The essential sanctity of the Holy Land is rooted in the Act of Creation. The Torah begins with the account of Creation to show that God created everything and that the Land is His, to give to whomever He desires. If the nations of the world claim that the Holy Land is theirs, the Jews can point to the Act of Creation; the world is God's and by His Divine Will He gave the Holy Land to the Jews (see Rashi, Genesis 1:1).

The sanctity of the Holy Land stems from the fact that God incorporated within Creation the intention and the potential for the Jews to conquer the Holy Land, thereby revealing His Kingdom. In this sense, the sanctity of the Holy Land is rooted in the "Ten Sayings," in the Concealed Torah, and in the *derekh eretz* — all of which are facets of the Treasury of Unearned Gifts which sustains life when people are not connected to Torah. Thus, the *derekh eretz* in which is concealed the Treasury of Unearned Gifts also refers to "*derekh* to *Eretz*," the pathway to the Land, the Holy Land — for *derekh eretz* refers to the Treasury of Unearned Gifts, which is synonymous with the sanctity of the Holy Land!

*

"Va'Etchanan" — *Moses' plea*

Rebbe Nachman now reviews this lesson in the context of Moses' prayer to God, "*Va'Etchanan* — I pleaded to God at that time."

Moses, in his plea to enter the Holy Land, asked God to grant him the permission he sought as a favor from the Treasury of Unearned Gifts. "I pleaded to God" — this refers to the Treasury of Unearned Gifts. "At *that* time" — refers to that *specific* time when the world was sustained exclusively by God's lovingkindness, granted through the concealed

Torah. For the pathway to the Land of Israel is paved with the power of God's lovingkindness inherent in Creation, which is the basis for the Treasury of Unearned Gifts.

*

What does all this mean to me?

The ideas represented in this lesson parallel Rebbe Nachman's conversation prior to giving this discourse. The Rebbe had said he was an "ordinary person," and that he drew inspiration only from his travels to the Holy Land. As we have seen, the path to the Holy Land reflects God's lovingkindness, indicating the Treasury of Unearned Gifts which has always sustained the world. Thus the tzaddik, when he is forced to interrupt his devotions for a few moments and thereby become an ordinary person, is still connected to the Treasury of Unearned Gifts and can interact with other "ordinary people," so that they too will be sustained. The closer a person is to the tzaddik, the more powerful is the life force that he can draw from the Treasury of Unearned Gifts. On the surface, this lesson seems to be speaking specifically about the tzaddik who, when he turns into a "commoner," can draw upon the Treasury of Unearned Gifts and thereby act as an interface between the Torah, which is the source of life, and the ordinary folk.

But a person may ask one very basic question: "What does all this mean to me?" It seems as though Rebbe Nachman was talking to himself, or about himself, or about people on very high spiritual levels. What practical application does this lesson have for me — the "ordinary person"?

Never despair!

After imparting this lesson, Rebbe Nachman began to speak freely with his followers about some of the concepts presented. He spoke about ordinary people — those who are overly busy with their livelihoods; and he spoke about those who do not know how to study Torah. He also spoke of those who are very distant from God, those who are engulfed in the quagmire of materialism. He alluded to himself, who was physically broken, and to others like himself; and he also discussed those who feel lost, emotionally haunted or spiritually starved. And he said:

"Never despair! There is always hope!"

"Despair does not exist!"

The Rebbe then explained that the Treasury of Unearned Gifts, the concealed Torah which sustained the world when the Torah was not yet formally revealed, is *always* present in this world. It is available to us through the tzaddik who draws upon that Treasury of Unearned Gifts to sustain all those multitudes who fall into the broad category of "common, ordinary people." No matter how low a person has descended, even if he has fallen to the lowest depths of existence where despondency and despair overwhelm him, he must remember: "Despair does not exist!" He can draw strength and inspiration, for since there is no such thing as despair, there is always hope! "Never despair!" For even in the darkest moments of life, the concealed Torah is always present to sustain a person. One *can* always draw upon God's limitless Treasury.

Rebbe Nachman then spoke about the great value of simplicity — for, as has been explained, the Treasury of Unearned Gifts is manifest only through the straightforwardness of the ordinary person. Generally, people tend to rationalize their lives, behavior and attitudes, citing various sophisticated ideas, and these "paths of thought" have complicated their lives. Sophisticated philosophies have too many "intersections," and they all too often mislead people; when caught in a web, people can rarely see or sense the correct, direct path out of their difficulties. The Rebbe always advised people to steer clear of sophisticated lifestyles, for they are convoluted paths. It is better to seek simple, straightforward paths, the path of the "ordinary person," the path of hope, the path from which one can always draw upon the Treasury of Unearned Gifts.

Rebbe Nachman concluded his lesson with the verse, "Fortunate is he who walks in the path of simplicity"(Psalms 119:1).

*

Rebbe Nachman's lesson introduces us to the awesome greatness of the Treasury of Unearned Gifts and shows us how, from the beginning of Creation, it has permeated every facet of life, sustaining a person even in his darkest moments. Once we understand the far-reaching scope of this Treasury, the Rebbe's message of "Never despair!" becomes a tangible force applicable to every one of us. In the remainder of this work, we will present several of Reb Noson's discourses on this subject, illustrating how the Treasury of Unearned Gifts is available to all of us and how easy it is for a person to draw from it and to live a contented, happy and rewarding life.

This Treasury is there for the asking. It is there for the one who pleads, "*Va'Etchanan* — I plead to You, God. Grant me a gift from Your Treasury of Unearned Gifts."

* * *

4

Give thanks for the past…

Rebbe Nachman's lesson expounding the Treasury of Unearned Gifts is based on the word *Va'Etchanan,* which is an expression of prayer. Prayer is the single basic means by which we may draw from that Treasury.

> "A person should always begin his prayers with praises of God; afterwards he should pray [for his needs]."
>
> *Berakhot* 32a

The Talmud teaches that we learn this from Moses. Moses pleaded, *"Va'Etchanan,"* entreating God to allow him to enter the Holy Land. But before he began beseeching God, he first praised Him (see Deuteronomy 3:23-25).

Logically this seems a direct enough approach. After all, when asking a favor from another person we usually lead up to the subject, rather than blurting out a blunt request. It is generally a more respectful way of doing things. Thus, we first praise God, singing His praises and thanking Him for the past good we have received. Then we begin our supplications, asking Him to grant our requests.

Reb Noson elucidates this concept in greater depth.

God knows each person's thoughts. He knows what everyone wants. Why must we pray? Though God is always sending down His bounty, it is incumbent upon each individual to create a vessel within which to receive this bounty. That vessel is created by the person's speech — through his prayers. Thus the verse states (Deuteronomy 1:11), "God will bless you *ka'asher diber lakhem*, as He has promised you." *Ka'asher diber lakhem* also translates as, "As your speech is," indicating that God's promise of bounty is carried out according to man's speech/prayer (Likutey Halakhot, Nachlot 4:3).

Reb Noson explains at length how God created the world in a way which requires man to determine his own destiny. Man, by virtue of his deeds, can affect the bounty he receives. This is understood from the verse (Genesis 2:3), "...which God *bara la'asot* — created and did (literally, "created to do"). This verse tells us that if man were to do his job properly, as he was meant to do, he could bring the world to its ultimate state of perfection. Thus, man's prayers *are* man's doing — it is man's desires and thoughts that bring him to recognize his Creator, and then to pray to Him. It is these prayers which create the vessel in which to receive God's bounty, because one who prays is *facing* God, and is thereby able to receive His blessings.

But these vessels remain incomplete until they are complemented by another factor, which is *faith*. A person must have faith in his prayers: faith in the belief that God created the entire world, that He rules over it and that everything depends on Divine Providence. A person must also have faith in himself: faith that God listens to every single word, every single letter, of his prayers. Every person is very special to God and God listens to him; and because each and every person is so important, man has power to "influence" God to grant his entreaties. This is why it is necessary to first praise God before praying for one's needs. If someone lacks complete faith in God, his prayers cannot be perfect; he lacks faith that God is Omnipotent and he lacks faith that his prayers will be listened to and can be effective. His prayers will be stagnant and he will feel unfulfilled. Conversely, when a person praises God, he finds that his faith is strengthened for, were this not so, why would he be praying to God at all? By praising God, the person connects with Him and feels that there is Someone to talk to, Someone Who *will* listen to him and grant his requests. Reb Noson continues:

> This is evident in the opening blessing of the *Amidah* prayer (*Sh'mona Esrei*, the 18 Benedictions), from our daily services. We begin by praising God, focusing first upon the Patriarchs, continuing with several additional praises and then mentioning "*gomel chasadim tovim*" (Who does many acts of kindness). We refer in a general sense to God's acts of kindness to remind us that the Patriarchs continually prayed to God and He answered them. Our faith is thus strengthened by the realization that God will hear and answer our prayers as well. This thought pervades the blessing which concludes, "He brings salvation to their descendants..." — because the answer to our prayers

is God's beneficence, which through our prayers, will become available to all generations.

We see that praising God is more than simply glorifying His name. It is in itself a system whereby we strengthen our faith in God. And, perhaps in an even deeper sense, praising God can instill in the individual the faith that he himself is important and plays a significant role in God's Master Plan. Thus, the more we praise God, the stronger becomes our faith.

*

Prayer and Faith

The vicissitudes of life are daunting and we need every grain of faith we can muster in order to live a life of contentment. But how can a person who is racked by doubts — about God, about himself, his livelihood, his friends, etc. — find contentment? He is continually beset with uncertainty and distrust and every step he takes along the pathways of life is a troubled one. Questions will continually haunt him: "Who will be next? What next? Why me?..." and so on. There is no denying that we all have good days and bad days. Yet, equipped with a strong faith, we can enjoy the good when it comes and face the bad with equanimity.

As we have pointed out, the way to attain faith is through prayer. Prayer builds up both our trust in God and our faith in ourselves. Faith thus becomes our bulwark in the face of difficulties. "God will see us through this trouble as He has in the past. Let us never allow ourselves to become overwhelmed." Even when faced with severe difficulties, one may strengthen that faith still more, with additional prayers for salvation.

Faith, as mentioned above, is another integral part of the vessel through which we can receive bounty. We form that vessel through our prayers. When we pray, we demonstrate faith that our prayers have meaning. When the answer to our prayers materializes, we are better equipped to accept that answer, for our prayers have strengthened our faith, and our faith has strengthened our prayers. People are often blessed with sudden windfalls, but, not having expected them, they squander the opportunity to take advantage of them. Other times, the windfall might be too big for them to handle — they don't have a vessel "large enough" to contain those blessings and their good fortune gets lost along the way. These are examples of bounty which is lost or misdirected, because the recipient is lacking in prayer, in faith, or in both. But with faith, one may have confidence that everything will work out, that troubles will be overcome and that the good might become even better!

The more a person prays, the more he sees answers to his prayers. This in itself strengthens his faith and encourages him to pray more, which in turn strengthens his prayers, which brings him to a greater sense of fulfillment. After all, "I've seen the answer to my prayers!"

*

King David and Avshalom

> "One should give thanks to God for the good one has already received, and cry out for success in the future."
>
> *Berakhot* 54a

This teaching of our Sages, "Give thanks for the past and cry out for the future," is crucial to our understanding of the relationship between prayer, faith and the Treasury of Unearned Gifts. It became a pivotal feature of King David's plea for salvation when his son Avshalom (Absalom) rebelled against him and usurped his kingdom (2 Samuel 15-18). King David was forced to flee, and while fleeing insult was added to injury: he encountered Shim'iy ben Geira of the tribe of Benjamin, a leading judge, who cursed him and humiliated him in public. Other troubles besieged him and it seemed as though his whole life was falling apart. His suffering was so great, that some of our Sages opine that he even considered idolatry! (*Sanhedrin* 107a).

During his flight, King David sang out to God (Psalms 3:1-2): "A psalm to David, when he fled from Avshalom, his son. God! My troubles are great...." Our Sages ask (*Berakhot* 7b): "'A *psalm* for David?' Shouldn't this be 'A *lamentation* for David'?!" His son had rebelled and King David was fleeing for his life! But King David found hope in the very fact that it was Avshalom, his own son, who was the main cause of his woes. King David recalled that, in general, a son will take pity on his father. Therefore, even in the midst of his deep troubles, he was able to draw strength and sing, rather than bemoan his fate. Things are not always as bad as they seem.

Reb Noson, in a most interesting approach, explains this incident in depth and shows how the lessons gleaned from it apply to each of us at all times. His discourse in its entirety is found in *Likutey Halakhot, Kila'ey Beheimah* (4:6).

> What could have been going through King David's mind at that time? What realization brought him to *sing* over his son's rebellion? Furthermore, what kind of song was it, since the psalm itself does not even speak of his salvation, but only of his deep trouble?

> King David found himself in very bitter straits. The most painful aspect of his troubles was the knowledge that the rebellion he now faced was punishment for his having taken Batsheva. Acknowledging his guilt, he cried out (Psalms 3:3), "Many say of me, 'He has no salvation from God'." King David was in such a state of depression and confusion that he could not even express himself properly before God and pray for his own salvation. What was he to do?

> At that point King David began to recall all the kindnesses he had received and the many and varied salvations he had experienced throughout his life. He began to remember all the good things, large and small, that had happened to him throughout all his sufferings — and there had been many. He felt that, even in the midst of this terrible trouble, with his own son leading the rebellion against him, surely there must be some kindness that he could find here as well. After all, there had been many, many times when he had suffered, "yet it always could have been worse." He realized that in every type of suffering he had endured in the past, there had always

been great kindnesses that God had provided to sustain him. Thus King David began to sing to God, to praise Him for all the good he had experienced throughout his lifetime, and he found that, even in the tragedy of his son's rebellion, he could discover a good point: "A son will take pity on his father." The realization that things weren't as dark as they seemed was a great relief to King David. He was then able to open his heart and pour out his prayers, "But You God are a shield for me...."

Reb Noson applies this incident in King David's life to each and every person, as the depression and confusion King David experienced is the universal response of those beset by many afflictions. They lose heart and lose hope, as if there were no way to overcome their difficulties. Their mouths are closed, they cannot pray. Some even feel anger at God because of their sufferings. But man never loses his freedom of choice and God always sends His "free gifts" according to His system of evaluation of what each person should receive. What determines the difference is the *attitude* of the person who receives God's bounty. Observe people who merit wealth, health, children and so on. Some appreciate their good fortune and thank God for it: they are charitable and will always use God's gifts to try to draw closer to Him. Others, upon receiving their good fortune, become arrogant and unbearable, thinking that they were blessed because they are worthy people and deserve it. On the other hand, when people receive a measure of suffering, some accept it as yet another means by which to draw nearer to God, while others become bitter and, because of their suffering, turn further away from Him.

If we examine King David's Book of Psalms, we find that many psalms contain this idea. The book is called *TeHILim*, from the word *TeHILah*, which means praise to God. Yet most of the book comprises cries and prayers aroused by King David's sufferings. King David teaches us through his psalms that life is full of trials and tribulations. The only way to maintain one's equilibrium through troubled times is to recall the good moments, to remember God's kindnesses and thereby to find solace, even when one must endure suffering.

Indeed, one cannot find solace in the midst of suffering without the hope of a future salvation. But how does one know that salvation is near? One can count on imminent salvation only by recalling the kindnesses and good times of the past. When a person examines his life till today and realizes how many difficult times there have been, remembering how help did arrive, he can be assured that there are more of God's kindnesses, from His Treasury of Unearned Gifts, awaiting him now and in the future.

As we have seen (Chapter 3), the Treasury of Unearned Gifts emanates from God's lovingkindness. The main gift that a person can receive from this Treasury is the ability to *experience* God's kindness. By recalling the good times, by reliving them, we draw upon the kindnesses that we have already experienced from God's Treasury of Unearned Gifts. We can know that this Treasury is always there for us; we can find comfort from suffering and always look forward with hope to better days to come.

*

Faith

"Without faith, one has no life."

Rabbi Nachman's Wisdom #52; *ibid.* #102

We have seen how prayer and faith are interrelated, and how together they bring a person to fuller appreciation of all that he experiences. Rebbe Nachman takes this a step further and explains that, without faith, one's life can be a truly bitter experience, with nary a hope for the future.

> A person who has faith can *always* experience a good life. Even if he must endure suffering, he realizes that it all comes from God, and that God's intention is always for his benefit. He can always find hope throughout his suffering. "Perhaps this suffering was sent to cleanse me of my sins," "Perhaps this suffering is to prepare me for a brighter future," and so on.

> But one without faith has no life — for life is full of suffering. When suffering visits, this person has nowhere to turn for comfort. It is obvious to everyone that This World is full of suffering. No one is exempt; no one. It is impossible for everything to go according to one's will. Thus, without faith, one's life is full of suffering, with too many complications and disappointments. Life becomes full of anger, pain and frustration.

Rebbe Nachman invested much energy into instilling faith in his followers. He once said (*Rabbi Nachman's Wisdom* #33), "The world considers faith a minor matter, but I consider it to be extremely important. The main pathway to faith is devoid of all sophistication and philosophical speculation. The greatest faith is the innocent faith of the ordinary person."

Without faith, one faces the vicissitudes of life without any pillar of support. With faith, a person can always find solace and joy, despite the most severe suffering he may endure. This is because faith enables one to seek God, to seek His kindness — and to find it. Thus, one with faith can always draw upon those resources found in such abundance in the Treasury of Unearned Gifts.

* * *

5

Think positive

In his discussion of prayer presented earlier (Chapter 4), Reb Noson points out the importance of having faith in oneself. With the emotional highs and lows that everyone experiences throughout life, it might be very easy to gain that faith — as well as to lose it. One might experience both highs and lows on a daily basis, and each day fluctuate between feeling confident and feeling down and out. Facing each day with a positive outlook and maintaining that optimism throughout calls for tremendous inner strength, but it is the *only* way to come through each day feeling content. Positive thinking is the single most important key to attaining contentment and happiness.

Happiness: the key to good living. How we all long for it! But this greatly coveted attribute of happiness will elude us unless we realize that its attainment demands being content with what we *have*, not with what we *want* (as above, Chapter 1). When I learn to take advantage of the treasures that I have — the treasure that I *am* — and to feel satisfied, then I am walking on the path of good living. The way to attain this life of satisfaction is to recognize the "gifts" that we live with constantly and to draw inspiration from that Treasury of Unearned Gifts.

*

Rebbe Nachman recognized the importance of positive thinking even in his time, and he often spoke about it. As was his custom regarding all concepts he deemed important, he addressed this idea in one of his lessons (*Likutey Moharan* II, 10).

> Know that one who is depressed cannot control his thinking as he desires. It is therefore very difficult for him to settle his mind. But through joy, one can gain control of one's mind. Joy represents the World of Freedom, as expressed in (Isaiah 55:12), "You will go out [from exile] with joy." This verse tells us that it is joy that brings the freedom through which one can leave the exile.

Any form of exile is a type of bondage. When a person is forced to live in unfavorable conditions, away from his comfortable surroundings, that is a kind of bondage. An unsatisfactory life is clearly a form of exile, for it places a person in bondage to the depression that constantly hovers over him. One who succumbs to depression is living with a "slave mentality"; he goes through the same motions as a "free person," but he lacks control of his life and his destiny. Conversely, joy is freedom. It is a state of mind wherein one feels in control, one feels confident, one enjoys contentment with one's situation or direction. One must therefore constantly strive to free oneself from exile and to seek living conditions which are conducive to joy. Rebbe Nachman continues:

To attain joy, a person must look for the positive points in his life. He must seek and discover all positive points that he may have. Upon finding the positive points, he can attain joy, for he now has much to be happy about.

The idea of searching for one's positive points is one of the most important lessons that Rebbe Nachman ever gave, and is known among Rebbe Nachman's followers as *Azamra!* — "I will sing" (*Likutey Moharan* I, 282). We will review parts of that lesson here in the context of our topic, the Treasury of Unearned Gifts.

*

In the courtrooms of the mind

Rebbe Nachman taught:

Know! One must judge every person favorably (cf. *Avot* 1:6). Even if someone is a complete sinner, one must seek to discover within him some good point which redeems him from being totally wicked. Through finding some modicum of good in a person and judging him favorably, one actually confers merit upon that person and can bring him to repentance.

People always have some reason for the things they do (even for things done impulsively). Whether it is valid or not, they have a reason for what they have done; whether their logic is right or wrong, they have a reason for what they did. And they think — at least most of the time — that they did the right thing. Nobody is a mind reader, nobody can know why anyone else did what he did. Since most people are basically decent and generally try to do the right thing, why should anyone judge another's deeds unfavorably? Even if someone said or did the wrong thing, most likely he had good intentions.

The tendency to make negative judgments is a major problem afflicting society and is a powerful contributing cause of unhappiness and discontent. Reb Noson explains that most disputes arise when a person feels that someone has insulted him or not shown him due respect (*Likutey Halakhot, Chovel b'Chaveiro* 3:3). In some instances, this evaluation might be true. But perhaps, just perhaps, the offending statement wasn't meant to embarrass the person or otherwise hurt him. However, people who have been hurt in some way tend to become both judge and jury; the offender is indicted and convicted, and now justice must be carried out. Anger, strife and any number of negative feelings then possess a person and destroy any tranquility he might otherwise have enjoyed.

Rebbe Nachman teaches that the approach of judging others favorably is a key component of a contented life. This may be borne out simply by asking oneself, "What do I *really* stand to gain from negativity or confrontation?" More than just a noble idea, judging others favorably has the power to combat negative feelings when they arise. The matter can be laid to rest and the person can anticipate a general feeling of tranquility.

Rebbe Nachman then takes this idea in a new direction.

A person must always judge *himself* favorably. One must always be happy and distance oneself from depression. Reflecting on one's life, one might find oneself lacking in attainments. This individual has judged himself unfavorably and has found himself lacking. He is full of remorse and self-pity: "This is lacking, that is blemished...." Nevertheless, he must continually strengthen himself — again and again — and must never allow himself to sink into depression. He must search and search, over and over if need be, for every good point he may possess. Upon finding his good points, a person finds merit in himself. He has some good; he has more than just *some* good. In this way he can attain joy.

With the pressures of life bearing down on each of us, it is all too easy to sink into depression and self-pity: "I'm not that good," "I've done wrong," "Others are far better than I am," "I have no future," and so on. Criticizing oneself is quite common and Rebbe Nachman points out that, when someone knocks himself down, it is difficult for him to get up again. It takes a huge amount of effort and great inner strength to continually build one's self-confidence. This awesome feat can be accomplished by searching one's past for good deeds, and by *finding* that good; for every one of us has certainly done some good in the past.

This is akin to drawing from the Treasury of Unearned Gifts. We've done some good in the past, but it has already been forgotten. However, that good is stored away somewhere in the recesses of our minds. It has only to be recalled and drawn forth. As we have seen, God's kindnesses are always sustaining us, even at times when we may not be worthy of them. In similar fashion, our own good can also sustain us — for it is only God Who gave us the ability to do that good to begin with. Thus, the good we have performed in the past is still available to us, and we can draw strength and inspiration from it at all times. Out of this substantial Treasury, we *can* always find ways of bringing joy into our lives. We can discover that, after all, we are worthy; we can find that we are better people than we had imagined. Of course there is always room for improvement, but viewing ourselves positively makes it easier to achieve a life of fulfillment.

*

Forget it!

Rebbe Nachman once said:

> "Most people think of forgetfulness as a defect. But I think it greatly beneficial. If we did not forget, it would be utterly impossible to serve God. We would remember our entire past, and these memories would drag us down and would not allow us to raise ourselves to spiritual heights. All our endeavors would be constantly defeated by the weight of our memories.
>
> "God gave us the power to forget and thus disregard the past. It is gone and never need be brought to mind. We can thus move on without being haunted by our past…. The best advice is simply to forget. As soon as something is behind us, we should forget it completely and never call it to mind again" (*Rabbi Nachman's Wisdom* #26).

This is another crucial point to bear in mind when searching for a life of contentment. Along with seeking the good points, and recalling them when we need to strengthen ourselves, we must forget our errors so that they do not drag us into depression and self-pity. This is easier said than done. Even if we wish to forget our mistakes, there are those who are only too eager to remind us of them. Not surprisingly, those people may often be none other than ourselves. Furthermore, it may be argued that there are certain benefits to remembering our wrongdoings. If we forget our mistakes, we won't be able to learn from them. Also, the Talmud speaks of the value of recalling one's sins, for then one's heart remains broken before God (*Yoma* 86b). This is a very important means of attaining spirituality. Still, there is no contradiction between the Rebbe's words and the talmudic statement, because Rebbe Nachman is referring to the *negative* implications of remembering our past deeds. He himself recommends that we remember things that benefit our spiritual growth. In the main, we are better off if we use our powers of recall to remind ourselves of our positive experiences.

Rebbe Nachman compares one trapped in painful memories to a blind person: sometimes he relies on a person with sight, and trusts him to guide him properly; at other times he depends on his own cane to guide him. The same is true of a person who feels depressed and overwhelmed, who feels entrapped in emotional darkness with no visible means of escape. Perhaps we can't see any way out of our troubles. But Rebbe Nachman advises us to remember, "there have been good times in the past," "there were occasions when I felt good." This will help us to have faith that more good awaits us in the future (*Likutey Moharan* I, 222).

Drawing on one's good points can alter one's negative attitude and can even transform it into positive thinking. This is because drawing on one's own treasury of goodness is comparable to drawing from the Treasury of Unearned Gifts. We can recall God's kindnesses and *know* that there is more good in store for us. Searching the past for any good we have done can provide us with great hope for the future.

*

The golden calf

Reb Noson illustrates the value of forgetting and relates it to the Treasury of Unearned Gifts in the context of the biblical account of the sin of the golden calf. It was when Moses had ascended on High to receive the Torah and the Jews thought they were without a leader that they made a golden calf. When he descended from Heaven with the Torah, Moses saw the calf and broke the Tablets upon which were inscribed the words of the Torah. Interestingly, the Talmud teaches that God actually applauded Moses for this act! (*Shabbat* 87a).

Reb Noson writes that the entire theme of Moses breaking the Tablets and God's subsequent approval is a very deep mystery: What could have possessed Moses to break the Tablets? The fact that the world was created for the sake of the Torah, and cannot exist without it, intensifies the question. The answer can be found in Rebbe Nachman's teaching regarding the Treasury of Unearned Gifts (above, Chapter 3).

When Moses descended Mount Sinai, he saw the golden calf and realized the gravity of the Jews' sin. Just 40 days earlier, God had appeared to them and had given them the Torah. In so short a period they had succumbed to the sin of idolatry. God's judgment against them demanded nothing less than their annihilation, for the Torah clearly states that idolaters deserve the death penalty. Thus, if the Jews now were to be given the Tablets, they would be guilty of idolatry and punished accordingly. Moses realized this dilemma and concluded that, to save the Jews, he must draw on a power that transcends Torah law. The power he found is God's Lovingkindness, the Treasury of Unearned Gifts, that had sustained the world until then. It is for this reason that Moses broke the Tablets. Reb Noson explains:

> This discussion is alluded to in Rebbe Nachman's lesson *Va'Etchanan*, where he explains that the tzaddik becomes an "ordinary person" when he interrupts his devotions. Moses had just received the Torah, having been taught it firsthand by God during 40 days he spent on Mount Sinai. Still, Moses broke the Tablets — he "forgot" his studies — by breaking his connection to the Torah and transforming himself into an "ordinary person." When the tzaddik becomes an ordinary person, he draws upon that Treasury of Unearned Gifts that sustained the world even when there was no Torah. (Even today, when so many people are so very distant from Torah, this Treasury is always available.) Moses, by breaking the Tablets, "caused" God to open His Treasury of Unearned Gifts and through it to

forgive the Jews for their sin. This is the reason God approved of Moses' deed, for God always seeks to bring to the world forgiveness and mercy (*Likutey Halakhot, Bet Knesset* 5:28).

Reb Noson continues that this same approach can be applied by each and every person throughout his life. Man experiences countless difficulties during the course of his lifetime. Many people have not stood up to the pressures of life and have fallen, each in his own way. The most effective way to remain strong when feeling overwhelmed is to act simply — to be an ordinary person and to forget all the evils of the past. Begin anew each time, draw upon the Treasury of Unearned Gifts, the Lovingkindness of God that permeates all of Creation due to the merit of the tzaddik, the extraordinary "ordinary person," who continually draws upon that treasury and makes it available to everyone. As an "ordinary person," one can always draw vitality — forever; because "God's Lovingkindness never ceases; His compassion never ends"(Lamentations 3:22).

* * *

6

In control or controlled?

It is frequently assumed that nothing is accomplished unless one "forces the issue." Ostensibly, this often seems to be the case. But it is certainly true that the benefits of forcing an issue are generally offset by side effects, many of which prove detrimental. We have already seen how prayer, faith, joy and the building of one's self-confidence are positive influences on one's life. In this chapter, we will explore the virtue of patience, as well as the importance of overcoming such negative characteristics as anger and arrogance.

Reb Noson points out the complexity of setting goals, and yet not forcing an issue. One who seeks that delicate balance walks a very fine line. Everyone must set goals and strive to accomplish them. On the other hand, one must be very careful not to force the issue because, even if one does succeed in attaining the goal, the damage caused by trying to exert too much control can often outweigh the gain. Reb Noson's discourse on this topic is based on one of Rebbe Nachman's lessons which discusses the episode of Moses striking the rock to obtain water for the Jewish Nation.

During the Jews' forty-year sojourn in the desert, a rock accompanied them which, when they encamped, transformed into a well and provided them with water. It was one of the miracles (along with the manna and the Clouds of Glory) that the Jews witnessed every day in the desert. When Miriam passed away, the rock's well dried up. God told Moses to take his staff, gather the people and *speak* to the rock so that it would give forth water. But there were those who challenged Moses and doubted him. "Could Moses indeed bring forth water from a rock?" they asked, for they knew that it was only due to Miriam that water had flowed from the well. Goaded by the Jews' arguments, Moses' patience snapped and, in his anger, he struck the rock. Because of this response, Moses passed away in the desert and never entered the Holy Land (Numbers 20 and see Rashi).

Rebbe Nachman taught:

> In order to disseminate Torah teachings that will instill within people the desire to serve God, one must develop words that are "hot as coals," that is, words that inspire. Before delivering a lesson, one's warm words should flow forth in prayer to open up the *tzur levavi*, the "rock of my heart" (i.e., God) (Psalms 73:26), and to draw "water" (Torah teachings) from that rock. Thus, before giving a lecture, a person must pray to God, asking that he be granted inspiring teachings; yet in his prayers, he must present himself as an impoverished pauper seeking a gift, rather than demanding a reward for his good deeds. One must always appeal to God, asking Him for a gift [of

teachings] from His Treasury of Unearned Gifts (*Likutey Moharan* I, 20).

A well in Hebrew is *B'ER*, which is related to the Hebrew word *BaER*, meaning "to explain." As we have just seen, one who wishes to "draw water from the well," to acquire Torah knowledge and impart it to others, must pray to God and request insight into Torah teachings. Rather than rely on his own merits, he should pray that God grant him the necessary knowledge as an unearned gift. In the biblical account mentioned above, the Jews were "thirsty" on the spiritual level as well, and they pressured Moses to provide them with Torah teachings. Moses did not stand in prayer as he should have, and did not derive the necessary teachings through supplication. Instead, he "raised his staff," indicating that he relied on his own strength, his own merits, to succeed, rather than on prayer and supplication. Instead of speaking to the rock, he forced the issue by striking the rock. He was meritorious enough to draw water through the strength of his good deeds, but on this occasion he did not achieve the noble and exalted goal of sanctifying God's Name. Drawing water from a rock through speaking to it would have sanctified God's Name far more than accomplishing the same feat through striking the rock — because it would have shown the importance of supplication as opposed to the use of force. In using force, Moses lost his chance to enter the Holy Land (which is symbolically the Treasury of Unearned Gifts; above, Chapter 3).

The important lesson to be learned from this, Rebbe Nachman taught, is that:

A person should never force an issue. Pray to God in supplication. If He answers, good. If He does not, accept it. But *never* force an issue.

*

Reb Noson explains (*Likutey Halakhot, Gezelah* 5) that Moses was well aware of the value of supplication. After all, he had used this type of prayer to win forgiveness for the Jews after the sin of the golden calf, as well as on various other occasions. Reb Noson focuses on several talmudic teachings about how Moses was pressured from without and thus came to err in striking the rock (cf. *Kohelet Rabbah* 7:7). He concludes that Moses was not as patient as he could have been. Similar incidents occurred several other times during his lifetime. In each case he was not totally at fault — but he lost patience and forced an issue. The consequences were very severe indeed.

This same misstep was also made by other biblical personalities with dire consequences. Because Abraham asked God (Genesis 15:8), "By what will I know...?" his children were sentenced to 400 years of bondage in Egypt. Reuben hastened to defend his mother's honor and lost his birthright. Simon and Levi rushed into battle with Shekhem to defend their sister's honor without asking Jacob's advice and were castigated. These and other instances are cited by Reb Noson. All these lapses are rooted in losing patience and "forcing an issue."

This lesson applies to every situation in which sin beckons. The evil inclination can be overwhelming at times. If one has the patience to "wait it out," one can succeed in conquering all one's evil traits. One must not lose patience, but must rather wait and wait. God on His part will take pity and will help that person.

This approach has great relevance to every area of life. We often find ourselves striving for certain goals: at home, at work, in our studies, in our relationships with others, in almost every facet of life. We should make every effort to attain those goals, for otherwise they may never be accomplished. But we often find ourselves pushing too hard when things appear to be going against us. Careful examination of our attempts to achieve a goal will ascertain whether we are striving for — or forcing — that goal. Reb Noson points out that, when striving to reach our target, we must carefully weigh our every move, especially when others are involved. And, he adds, the only real way to be sure that we are on the right track is by continuously praying to God to grant us a gift from His Treasury of Unearned Gifts and to enable us to reach our goals.

*

Tolerance vs. temper

Patience is essential to living a good life. Patience is the principal ingredient that is required to ensure lasting relationships, mutual respect among people, attention to detail at home and at work, and dozens of other ideals. It creates security in one's life. Forcing an issue, on the other hand, is entirely different. Sometimes it may seem like the right thing to do: we must apply a certain amount of pressure, otherwise the job might never get done. However, when matters are forced, anger is rampant, tempers flare and, even if a job is in fact completed, very little good ever comes from an angry approach. Rebbe Nachman once remarked, "Anger never achieves anything. Even if one sees that one has accomplished something through anger, rest assured that with tolerance one would have accomplished far more."

Patience and tolerance are also important qualities for the attainment of faith. Faith involves believing that all that comes a person's way — even obstacles, confusion, opposition and the like — emanate from God. Thus, a person with faith must also be tolerant, exhibiting patience in the face of difficulty and suffering. He must even be patient when faced with his own lack of success, spiritual and material. No matter what he experiences, his faith will enable him to go forward and carry on with life (see *Likutey Moharan* I, 155).

This is in sharp contrast to the perpetually angry person, who is demanding and who lacks patience and tolerance. The Talmud teaches, "Whoever is angry, all types of Gehennom (hell) rule over him"(*Nedarim* 22a). This is not difficult to visualize, for anyone who is angry gets "hot under the collar" and everything annoys him — he is irritable and uncompromising — in short, he is suffering as if he was experiencing hell. He cannot tolerate what is happening around him or to him. He is insecure, and in his angry outbursts he displays his insecurity for all to see.

Conversely, patience leads to a feeling of security and contentment in life. A tolerant person can be confident of whom he is and of his station in life; he can be content with his possessions, with his social circle, even with his problems!

Our Sages state, "An angry person will attain only anger" (*Kiddushin* 41a). Rebbe Nachman explains that anger in Hebrew is *ChaiMaH*, while the similar Hebrew word, *ChoMaH*, translates as "a wall" — which implies a wall of security. One who becomes angry has transformed his *chomah* (security) into *chaimah* (anger). He loses his sense of security. An angry person loses his self-control, displaying his lack of security. He has sacrificed his wall of protection, his security, and is left emotionally defenseless. We do not need a great deal of imagination to recognize this truth: simply take note of how an angry person is viewed by others.

The verse (Exodus 6:9), "They would not listen to Moses, because they were short-winded [i.e., lacking in spirit] due to their hard labor," describes the Jewish People in their bondage. "Short-winded" indicates the anger of one who lacks patience. Rebbe Nachman elaborates on this theme (*Likutey Moharan* II, 86): The angrier the person, the harder he has to work. This is because, "They were short-winded, therefore they suffered with hard labor." This also shows the importance of the role of patience as it relates to becoming a contented person. One who has patience, and hence contentment, won't feel that need to become a "workaholic" in his efforts to guarantee financial security through force. He'll find contentment within *life* itself, rather than through hard labor.

*

Another important ingredient for a life of contentment is patience and tolerance for people who are different from oneself. This attitude results in mutual respect and lasting relationships. When presenting the lesson of *Azamra!*, finding the good points in ourselves and in others (see Chapter 5), Rebbe Nachman points out how important it is to see the good in everyone. This can be accomplished only if we are tolerant of others and of their views, even if those views are diametrically opposed to our own. Our personal views constitute a treasury of our own, one that offers *us* contentment, one with which we feel comfortable enough to live. But in the same way, so are the other person's views of *his* personal treasury. By accepting that there is a Treasury of Unearned Gifts, we can accept that each person's gifts are those granted to him by God through the circumstances and influences that helped form his life. If we can reach this level of acceptance then we *can* tolerate differences among people, and this tolerance allows us to practice patience with others.

Tolerating the beliefs of others is not at all easy. It calls for an open mind, one that is secure in its own approach to life and is not threatened by another's opinions. This does not imply that one has to agree with other people's points of view. It does mean that one's own security will not lead to strife. Reb Noson writes that everyone "knows" the truth. That is, everyone knows *his* truth, the way he sees it from his unique vantage point in life. But then, the other person also "knows" *his* truth, with full confidence. Thus, so long as you tolerate the "truth" of your fellow man, judging him favorably and assuming him to be as sincere in his path and views as you are in your own, then, despite your differences, you can remain friendly and on good terms with one another, secure in your relationship.

*

Truth, victory and control

The traits of patience and tolerance mentioned above must be applied to all facets of one's personality; they are not restricted only to the area of controlling one's anger. Indeed, the more a person is in control of all his characteristics and desires, the greater is the degree of control he wields over his life. Incorporating patience and tolerance in all aspects of life becomes crucial when we begin to realize the pressures that avarice, gluttony and immorality place upon our daily lives. The control we exercise in these areas allows us to control the quality of our lives in general, since controlling our negative traits automatically gives us a feeling of general security in life. However, the potentially positive characteristic of control is often abused and can lead to the craving to control others.

The power to control is very attractive — it seems easier to control others, and it helps to cover up one's own shortcomings. Psychiatrists and psychologists consistently cite the "need to control" as a harmful characteristic and as a leading cause of unbalanced living, both at home and at work. Rebbe Nachman recognized this two centuries ago and taught:

> There is a character trait that rejects truth. This flaw is the desire to be victorious. Even if one with this trait recognizes the truth, he will nevertheless reject truth in favor of victory (*Likutey Moharan* I, 122).

In these few words, Rebbe Nachman sums up several important ideas: truth, victory and control. Truth is unquestionably a major foundation for building a contented life. The Talmud teaches, "Truth endures, falsehood does not" (*Shabbat* 104a). Honesty makes for secure relationships — between husband and wife, among friends and neighbors, with business associates and so on. A truthful person will be honest in all his dealings with others, and one can feel confidence in any relationship with him.

But the character trait of "victory" rejects truth. One who feels the need to always be right seeks a means of "winning" over another in order that *his* argument, or *his* viewpoint, be accepted. It is perfectly reasonable to argue one's cause if one feels it is correct. But too often arguments degenerate, and are carried on simply for argument's sake, even after one party recognizes the validity of the other's view. Because of the desire for victory, many people cannot tolerate losing an argument or even acknowledging that another view might be correct. Such arguments often lead to anger; how can they ever bring minds together? The craving for victory is a complete contradiction to truth, honesty and security.

Intrinsic to the trait of victory is the craving to control and to impose one's views upon others. One who craves victory seeks to control others, although it may be contrary to truth, or even to one's own security. A person feels he must be recognized and accepted, he *must* emerge the winner. But this urge to control can result only in strife. Reb Noson illustrates this through a brief glance at history (see *Likutey Halakhot, Birkhot Peratiyut* 5:2).

In Hebrew, the word for victory is *NaTzaCH*, which is etymologically parallel to *NeTzaCH*, eternal. This teaches us that the only victory one should ever seek is that which can remain for eternity. The only such victory is the victory of one's good inclination over one's evil inclination, and over one's evil characteristics. All other "victories" result in losses.

Throughout history, kings and generals have fought and won countless battles, assuming power for a period of time, only to suffer a decisive defeat and relinquish their ruling positions at a later date. Upon losing a war, the general or king is humbled, often imprisoned and tortured. In some instances we find kings have won wars and successfully established their kingdoms but, after a generation or two, their descendants are conquered and their dynasty disappears. There have been entire royal families who were murdered in revenge. Are these then the rewards of victory? To conquer others and control their lives and destinies, only to be humiliated later? To be set upon by enemies? To be avenged and annihilated at a later date?

Similarly, even and especially on a personal scale, all victories that must be imposed upon others are not really victories at all. In fact, they are humbling and humiliating and detrimental to *life* itself. The only victory worthy of its name is one to which truth is integral, for "truth endures." One who seeks truth will always be victorious. He will always feel secure.

*

We must understand the dichotomy inherent within the concept of control. Contemporary behaviorism recognizes the negative ramifications of the trait of control when exercised over others. Furthermore, many of the same behavioral scientists who vehemently oppose exerting control over others, advocate a "letting oneself go" attitude when one feels like doing so. "It's all right to display anger and let off steam." "It's permitted to pursue unnatural lifestyles." It would seem from these popular views that, in our generation, one no longer has to exercise any self-control. And the result is a "carefree society" — but one in which just about everyone is harried and must search high and low for happiness and contentment.

Reb Noson's commentary on victory gives us a simple, straightforward understanding of the need to exercise control. What is important is to focus on victory for eternal life. We can begin by exercising control over our desire for excesses and immorality. Exercising restraint and practicing tolerance will lead to respect for others, not to control over them. As we have discussed, all this leads to contented living.

*

Truth and humility

We have touched upon the concept of truth as an essential element in building a secure life. Though this is self-explanatory, we can add a few more thoughts to place the idea in clearer perspective. The trait of humility, as opposed to arrogance and vanity, will also be reviewed in our presentation of Rebbe Nachman's recipe for better living.

"God is truth; He is a living God..." (Jeremiah 10:10).

There is one ultimate Truth: this truth is God. He exists everywhere. It is He Who placed us in our environment. He has overseen our growth and development which have led us to our current way of life and to our current situation. If one wishes to implant truth within one's life, to ensure that security will be part of one's life, then one must bring God into one's life.

How to go about doing this is what the entire Torah, Talmud, Midrash, Kabbalah and other Holy Writings are about. Everyone is free to choose whichever path suits him best when seeking Godliness. But as explained above in our discussion on faith (Chapter 4), "Without faith, one has no life." It is easy to understand how faith in God is the principal ingredient of a life of contentment. Here we present another important concept, that faith must be bound together with truth. This is crucial because faith in falsehood can only mislead a person and brings in its wake a shattered life. Anyone, in order to be content, must be honest, especially with himself.

One of the greatest assets to be found in one's personal Treasury of Unearned Gifts is the innate ability to *always* discern the truth (see *Likutey Moharan* I, 156). God granted each person the ability to *know*, deep in his heart, the real truth. Anyone can sense what the truth is at any given moment, and can strive to attain it. We must bear in mind that we constantly rationalize our deviations from the truth, and outright falsehoods are easily recognizable. Armed with truth, one can build solid foundations for a life of contentment. Without it, one builds one's life on weak foundations which can and generally do fall apart when difficulties strike.

King David states, "God is my light and my salvation..." (Psalms 27:1). God is "light," indicating that, with God, one has the ability to see clearly. By inference, without God, one is walking in "darkness," lacking the clarity necessary to define one's goals or one's direction in life. God, as *the* Light, is always there to illumine a person's life and help guide the person on the right path. The more seriously and intensely a person seeks truth, the closer he comes to God and the clearer is the perception he will have of how to *live* his life (see *Likutey Moharan* I, 9:3).

*

Truth is a greatly sought-after commodity, yet a most elusive one. One of the main obstacles to recognizing truth is haughtiness. Rebbe Nachman refers to arrogant people as "needy people," because they crave the recognition of others. As long as a person cannot be honest with himself and feels he must put on a show for others — at home, at his job, etc. — that person is "needy," and remains in a mode of "performing" for others (see *Likutey Moharan* I, 66:3).

The person who strives for humility, while seeking to be honest with himself, will recognize and accept his own shortcomings. This recognition alone is generally sufficient to help keep him on a balanced path, so that he can deal with and grow from the difficult moments, while enjoying the good times. However, one who is haughty thinks that everything is due him. When things go against his expectations, they grate upon him and he feels that he has been wronged. This person can never face adversity without losing his temper, or feeling that his "control" is waning. Rebbe Nachman addresses both these attitudes in the following manner:

There is *k'seider* (order) and there is *shelo k'seider* (disorder). Order implies an awareness of God's presence in our lives so that, whatever happens, we attach ourselves to God. Disorder results from excluding God from our lives, so that everything that happens to us goes against our will. Disorder may dominate a person's life because he considers himself important, thinking, "I can rule." He removes God from his life by feeling that he, and not God, rules. Humbling oneself and accepting God's authority lead to order in one's life (*Likutey Moharan* II, 82).

The character traits of craving victory and control go hand in hand with haughtiness. There can be no contentment in life when one is thrall to these evil characteristics. Throughout his teachings, Rebbe Nachman discusses the subjects of anger, arrogance, control and victory, exhorting those who would heed his advice to work on subduing these traits.

*

Rebbe Nachman also spoke of the three major lusts: avarice, gluttony and immorality — which rage within a person, almost without remission, throughout his life. Eating to gain strength can easily degenerate into senseless overeating; while one needs money to pay the bills, it is difficult to set limits on how much money to spend or how much to seek; and the sexual urge, so basic to the propagation of mankind, too often becomes a raging, all-consuming passion. These lusts, when they become overpowering, squander one's time, effort, health and wealth. Falling victim to even one of them has an adverse effect on a person's life.

But how can we avoid them? We must eat. We must pay bills. We are obligated to bring children into the world. Rebbe Nachman compares overindulgence in these lusts to Adam's eating from the Tree of Knowledge of Good and Evil. The Tree is so named because of the great amount of good that can be "plucked" from it, on the one hand, and the evil that lurks there, on the other. (It may seem that the parallel is not exact, for Adam was forbidden to eat from the Tree, while we are allowed to enjoy that which the Torah permits. The factor common to both situations is the recognition of limits and self-control.) Since we know that eating, having money and propagating are all beneficial to mankind, it is clear that they can't be inherently evil. Yet excess in any of these areas is *always* harmful. Therefore, one must seek a path of moderation. One must eat what is permitted and beneficial to one's health. Sexual relationships must be limited to those permitted by the Torah. One can aspire to wealth, but not at the expense of one's spiritual fulfillment, physical strength, or personal relationships.

*

Undesirable character traits and lusts are not at all easy to break. We are exposed to them, or they become habits, from childhood, and our attempts to overcome them are hindered by continual exposure to modern trends and mass media. How then can we expect to improve our lives? Rebbe Nachman's suggests that we employ our innate abilities, our own treasuries, for better living: always look for the good in others and in ourselves; always strive for joy; pray and pray again; strengthen our faith; and constantly seek the truth. The underlying logic here is that the more one is involved in doing good, the less time and energy, and the less inclination, one has to indulge in evil.

Thus the secret to contented living lies in always being occupied with good deeds, which leads to joy in life. Make others happy, make yourself happy. Force your happiness if need be, but be happy, in order to maintain a positive attitude. (This is not the same as "forcing an issue" as above, because forcing happiness means conditioning your own state of mind, and thus cannot be compared to forcing an issue.)

Never despair! Never give up hope! Strengthen your faith in God and recognize that He always wants only what is good for you. You might not understand Him and His ways — but then again, if you did, why would He be God?

Pray to God. Praise God for the past good that you've experienced. Revel in it; draw hope and joy from all the good moments you have experienced. Then, having achieved a positive frame of mind, you'll be able to properly cry out for the future. Your mind will be focused on your real needs, and this will enable you to concentrate on whatever requires your attention, in order to move forward in life.

Keep life simple. The less complicated you make your life, the easier it will be to face the daily challenges that arise. Although people sometimes find themselves in situations from which it is difficult to extricate themselves, a simple lifestyle allows people to be free — to be able to examine and explore with a clarity of mind any new situations that arise.

And always be honest — with yourself and with others. The Talmud tells of a young man who joined a band of thieves and murderers. He wanted to repent and sought advice from Rabbi Shimon ben Shetach. Realizing how difficult it would be to separate oneself from such a past, Rabbi Shimon offered the young man just one suggestion: always tell the truth. Afterwards, whenever he had to decide whether to do right or wrong, the young man always thought of Rabbi Shimon's advice. He asked himself, "If I am confronted, will I answer truthfully regarding this action?" Having committed himself to telling the truth, he found himself unable to do wrong or to hurt others. Conducting himself with truth completely transformed the young man's life. Such is the power of truth.

* * *

7

The "good life"

Rebbe Nachman was once speaking to his followers about life. "It isn't how long a person lives that counts," he said. "It is *how* he lives. One doesn't need to live long, but only to live *well*."

Considering that he died six months short of his 39th birthday, we can conjecture that Rebbe Nachman was commenting on his own life. If so, what did he mean by "living well"? In good health? In luxury? Rebbe Nachman had neither and his life was marked by continual suffering. Of his eight children, four died in infancy. His first wife passed away when he was just thirty-five. Though he had a steady income, Rebbe Nachman was by no means wealthy. Furthermore, he suffered physically, most notably in his later years, when he contracted tuberculosis. When Rebbe Nachman spoke of "living well," he certainly wasn't referring to his own life. Or was he?

To Rebbe Nachman, life is defined by Torah (as above, Chapter 3). Being attached to Torah means forging an attachment to life itself. God *is* life, and God is always good (cf. Psalms 145:9). Therefore, "living well" means being aware of

God at all times and making sure that God is an integral part of one's life. This can be accomplished through studying Torah and following its precepts. In this way one becomes attached to God and gains a truly good life. Rebbe Nachman demonstrates the truth of this idea in the context of one of our Sages' teachings (see *Rabbi Nachman's Wisdom* #308).

> This is the way of the Torah: Eat bread with salt, drink water by the measure, sleep on the ground and live a life of pain, and in Torah you should toil. If you do this, then "You are fortunate and good will be yours" (Psalms 128:2). You are fortunate in this world and good will be yours in the World to Come (*Avot* 6:4).

This Mishnah is quite difficult to understand. If someone lives on bread and water, sleeps on the ground and lives a life of pain, how can it be said that he is "fortunate"? Rebbe Nachman asks us to consider for the moment the terrible suffering that abounds in the world. Even the wealthy live with a fair share of suffering, not to mention all the worries that are an inevitable feature of worldly possessions and status. The poor certainly suffer. Thus, for both rich and poor, the world is full of pain and suffering. And how many suffer due to illness and accidents? There is no escape in this world — except through Torah.

Rebbe Nachman thus taught:

> If you desire the material good of this world and want to live at ease without troubles, you will be constantly frustrated. The more you seek this "good," the more you will find the opposite. Any good you do

manage to grasp will be diluted with suffering.
Observe life honestly and you will see this for yourself.
The only way to be at ease is to be willing to subsist on
an absolute minimum.

Firmly resolve to follow the dictum of the Mishnah,
"Eat bread with salt... live a life of pain." Accept
graciously any of life's hardships and afflictions in
order to devote yourself to the Torah, "and in Torah
you should toil." No longer will worldly misfortunes
prove to be a source of suffering to you. You have
already accepted them upon yourself for the sake of
Torah! Then all your life — all your good — will be the
true good. Thus, your life is a true life. Fortunate are
you....

Simply put, Rebbe Nachman advises us to be wise and
set our sights on a simple life. For one who realizes that this
world is full of suffering and pain knows that the "good life"
of this world is not really attainable in any case. One who
aims for a simple existence is not thrown off course when
faced with frustrations or obstacles. This person can truly
appreciate all the little things that come his way — which
bring joy and happiness into his life. Thus, Rebbe Nachman
advises, accept the way of Torah, "eat bread with salt...." Live
simply; don't fall prey to the "good" of this world, which
lures us with avarice, gluttony and immorality. Then you can
be truly happy and prosperous. "You are fortunate in this
world and good will be yours in the World to Come."

*

The fixer

To illustrate how a simple life can be so rewarding, Rebbe Nachman told the following story (see *Rabbi Nachman's Stories* #29, pp.485-489).

There was once a king who said to himself, "Who can have fewer worries than I? I have all that is good and I am a king and a ruler."

He set out to investigate this. He walked around at night, standing behind houses, and listening to what people were saying. At one house, for example, he heard that the owner had troubles, and had to obtain an audience with the king. In this way, he heard each one's complaints and worries concerning their business affairs and their private lives.

Then he saw a very low house. Its roof had fallen in and it was so sunken that its windows were literally at ground level. The king bent down to look through the window and saw a man playing the fiddle. He had to listen very hard to hear the sound. The man had food and wine in front of him. He appeared very happy, in fact full of joy and without any worries.

The king went into the house, asked how the man was managing and the man replied in a positive manner. The king saw the wine and the food in front of the man, and saw the joy on the man's face. The man gave the king some wine, and drank a toast to the king's health. Out of love, the king also drank.

Then, seeing that the man was totally happy, without any worries whatever, the king lay down to sleep. In the morning the king and the man arose.

"How do you get your food and drink?" asked the king.

"I am a repairman," replied the man. "I can fix anything that is broken. I can't make anything new, but I can fix things. I go out in the morning, and I fix things. When I have five or six gulden, I buy myself food and drink."

When the king heard this, he said to himself, "I will test him."

The king returned home and issued a decree that if anyone has anything broken, he should not give it to anyone to fix. He must either fix it himself or buy something new.

The next morning the fixer went out and looked for things to repair. He was told that the king had issued a decree that nothing be given to others to fix. This was bad for him, but he had trust in God.

He walked a while, and saw a wealthy man cutting wood. "Why are you cutting the wood yourself?" asked the fixer. "Isn't it beneath your dignity?"

"I tried to find someone to cut the wood for me," replied the rich man, "but I couldn't find anyone. I had no choice but to cut it myself."

"Let me," replied the fixer. "I will cut the wood for you."

He cut the wood, and the rich man gave him a gulden. He saw that this was a good way to earn money, so he went on cutting more wood, until he had earned six gulden. He took the money and bought himself his meal. The meal was a feast and he was very happy.

The king went out again that night, and stood outside the fixer's window to see what had happened. He saw the fixer sitting with food and drink in front of him, very happy. The king went in and, as on the previous night, they then went to sleep.

In the morning, the king asked the man, "Where did you earn money to buy food?"

"My usual work is to repair things," replied the fixer. "But the king made a law that nothing can be given to another to be fixed. So I went and chopped wood until I had enough money for what I needed."

After leaving the fixer, the king issued a decree that no one should hire anyone to cut wood.

When the man heard this, he was upset, since he had no money. But still, he trusted in God. He walked a while, and saw a man cleaning out his stable. "Who are you to be cleaning out a stable?" he asked.

"I looked all over, " replied the other, "and I couldn't find anyone to do it for me. Therefore, I had to do it myself."

"Let me," replied the fixer. "I will clean it out for you."

When he was finished the man gave him two gulden. He cleaned out a few more stables, and earned himself the six gulden that he needed. He bought his entire meal, and returned home. The meal was a feast for him, and he was very happy.

The king went out again to see what had happened, and again saw the man happy. The king came in, spent the night, and in the morning, the king asked him how he earned the money for food and drink. The fixer explained what he had done. The king then issued a decree that no one may be hired to clean out barns or stables.

That morning, the fixer went out to clean stables, but he was told that the king had made a law that no one be hired to do such work. Not having any choice, the fixer went to the recruiting officer and joined the national guard. (Some soldiers are drafted, but others work for pay.)

The fixer hired himself out as a soldier, on condition that he would join only on a temporary basis, and that the recruiting officer would pay him every day. He immediately donned his uniform, and girded his sword at his side. At night, he took off his uniform, and with his pay he bought himself his meal and went home. The meal was a feast for him, and he was very happy.

The king went to see what had happened. He saw that the fixer had everything he needed, and that he was very happy. He entered the house, and spent the night with him as before. The king then asked him how he was managing, and the fixer told him the whole story. The king ordered the officer not to pay any of the soldiers that morning.

When the fixer asked the officer for his daily wage the officer refused. The fixer said, "But we made an agreement that you would pay me every day." "True," replied the officer, "but the king decreed that no one may receive payment today."

The fixer pleaded and argued, but to no avail. "I'll pay you tomorrow for two days," said the officer. "But today it is impossible to pay you."

The fixer devised a plan. He removed the blade from his sword, and replaced it with a wooden blade, so that no one could tell the difference. He then pawned the sword's blade and bought his meal as usual. The meal was a feast.

The king came back and saw that the fixer was perfectly happy. He spent the night, and asked him how he was managing. The fixer told him the whole story, how he had removed the blade from the sword, and had pawned it to buy his meal. "When I get paid today," he finished, "I will redeem the blade and fix it. No one will know the difference. I can fix anything! The king will have lost nothing."

When the king returned to his palace, he summoned the officer in charge. He said, "I have a criminal who has been sentenced to death. Call this fixer whom you recruited as a mercenary, and order him to cut off this criminal's head."

The officer went and summoned the fixer. The king ordered that all the officers be present to see this joke. He told them that one of his soldiers had replaced the metal blade of his sword with a wooden one.

When the fixer came before the king, he fell on the ground before the king and pleaded, "Your Majesty. Why did you summon me?"

"To behead a criminal," replied the king.

The fixer begged and pleaded. "But I have never killed a man," he said. "Please! Order someone else to do it."

"That's just why I'm commanding you to do it," replied the king.

"Is the case really that clear?" asked the fixer. "Is there no shadow of doubt? Maybe he's innocent? I have never killed a man in my life. How can I now kill someone who might not even deserve to die?"

"There is no question whatsoever that he deserves to die," replied the king. "The verdict is unanimous. And you must be the one to carry out the sentence and execute him."

When the fixer saw that he could not dissuade the king, he raised his eyes heavenward and said, "God Almighty. I have never killed a person in my life. If this man does not deserve to die, let the blade of my sword turn to wood."

With that, he drew his sword, and everyone saw that the blade was a piece of wood. Everyone had a good laugh. The king saw what a fine man the fixer was, and he let him go home in peace.

*

When examining the character of the fixer, we find that he embodies Rebbe Nachman's recommendations for better living. His home was less than modest, his possessions meager. Yet he thought positively, retained his faith in the face of adversity, and he never despaired. He always strove for joy, keeping his life simple and within attainable boundaries. Even when his source of income was denied him, he did not despair. Rather he trusted that God would help him and he actively pursued new opportunities. And he didn't balk at having to find new work on a daily basis.

*

We can all achieve the *joie de vivre* of Rebbe Nachman's fixer, if we will but set our sights on a simple, straightforward life. God has an immense Treasury of Unearned Gifts which is abundantly available to all of us. It is God's "personal" Treasury, holding only goodness and kindness. God's desire is to reward from this Treasury anyone and everyone whom He sees fit. We can all profit from it, without having to wait until after our passing from this world. Just as God permeates all levels of Creation, His goodness is present on all levels. Therefore, we can reap the advantages of this storehouse of goodness even now. But how?

1) Through prayer: by establishing a set time to practice *hitbodedut* daily — private prayer and meditation, reviewing both our growth and our inhibitions. We can reflect upon difficult times we have experienced, draw strength from past positive experiences and integrate that strength into our present lives. We can then face the future with hope that, with God's help, there are even better times awaiting us.

2) By strengthening our faith: in God, in Torah, in the tzaddikim and in ourselves. We must grow more and more certain that we are beloved by God, that we *can* make the connection with Him and that each and every one of us plays a crucial role in God's overall scheme of Creation.

3) By seeking the good that abounds in ourselves and in others. When we learn to focus on the good, we are surrounded by good.

4) By being honest with ourselves: by not building our lives on false hopes and expectations but on the realities around us. With an honest approach to life we can make the most

advantageous use of our abilities. By being honest with others: in relationships, in finances, in all areas of life. Truth instills security in our lives and in our routines.

5) By embracing joy at all times: looking for joy, forcing ourselves to overcome the depression and the confusion that often threaten to overwhelm us. As we have seen, joy represents freedom (Chapter 5).

With joy we can become free people, free from the evil characteristics that would drag us down to the depths of melancholy. With happiness, we are free to choose the lifestyle we wish; we need not be trapped within the drudgery of a society that preaches a carefree life, but is actually enslaved to its own self-serving dictates.

With joy, we can take charge of our lives. "We can have our cake and eat it too." We can revel in the good that we have, in the continuous good that God grants us. We can look forward to reward for the good deeds we have performed, and we can experience the greater joy of knowing that we have sought — and found — good in this life.

We may rest assured that if we tried to pray and be happy, if we strove for truth and faith, even if we haven't attained the highest levels, we have at least, in some manner, experienced God. If we have deserved this blissful experience, then we have been generously recompensed. If not, then we have been granted yet another gift from God's Treasury of Unearned Gifts.

* * *

8

"And I pleaded"

Rebbe Nachman told his followers to "turn the lessons into prayers" (*Likutey Moharan* II, 25). His prescription was an expression of the intrinsic relationship between prayer and study in the spiritual life of the Jew. Study alone is insufficient because this gives us only the "potential" knowledge of God. We must translate our academic knowledge into tangible good deeds through which we can experience God. Prayer is the catalyst which transforms our studies and thoughts into "concrete" spirituality; it is the channel through which we beseech God to enable us to transform our newly-found knowledge into an actual experience of Godliness.

With the Rebbe's encouragement, Reb Noson composed elaborate prayers based on *Likutey Moharan* ("The Collected Teachings of Rebbe Nachman"). These prayers are presented in *Likutey Tefilot* ("The Collected Prayers"), many of which appear in English translation in "The Fiftieth Gate." Translations of others have been included in various books published by the Breslov Research Institute.

Following is Reb Noson's prayer based on Rebbe Nachman's lesson of *"Va'Etchanan* — And I pleaded," in which he beseeches God to grant him an allocation from the Treasury of Unearned Gifts (see above, Chapter 3). It is found in *Likutey Tefilot* II, Prayer #39. Reb Noson opens his prayer by quoting Moses' words of supplication that he be allowed to pass over the Jordan River and enter the Holy Land.

(Reb Noson's prayers are extremely moving and very poetic. Though he obviously concentrated upon the subject matter, Reb Noson would often weave into his prayers many biblical passages, which relate to the objectives of that prayer. Constant references to their sources would seriously interrupt the flow of the prayer and were thus omitted. This rendition also incorporates various talmudic interpretations of the verses quoted. As such, they are not always translated literally.)

*

"And I pleaded to God at that time, saying: God! You have begun to show Your servant Your greatness and Your mighty hand; is there any power in heaven or earth that can match Your feats? Allow me, please, to pass over and see the good earth that is across the Jordan: the good mountain and the Holy Temple."

Master of the Universe, Who is filled with compassion, Who is gracious to those who are unworthy and Who shows compassion to those who are undeserving, Who performs unearned lovingkindness in every generation. You have already done many kindnesses for the community and for individuals in each generation. To this day Your compassion has assisted us and Your kindness has not deserted us.

And even for me, lowly and despised as I am, You have done innumerable and inestimable kindnesses and favors. "Were my mouth filled with song as the oceans, my tongue filled with melodies as the waves of the sea..." my life would not be long enough to praise, laud, extoll, bless and sanctify You, to thank You for, and enumerate, even one of the many thousands upon thousands, millions upon millions of the favors, miracles, wonders and kindnesses — all unearned — that You have done for me from the day I was born until this very day.

What can I say? What can I say? What merit can I claim for myself before God? How can I submit to the Most High? For which Unearned Gift of Your Treasury that You have lovingly granted me shall I thank You first? Every kindness that You have done for me, sinner that I am, is an abundant treasure from You, an unearned gift. For in Your great kindness You have strengthened me with yearning for Your faith, and You have granted me the privilege of being a Jew, one of Your chosen servants.

You always help me to snatch from this passing world many, many good points: Every day You grant me the merit to study some Torah and to pray a little; to fulfill some mitzvot and to keep away from sins. You helped me to avoid following the advice of the wicked, standing among sinners, and joining groups of cynics. You caused me constantly to yearn, long and pine for You, to associate with fine people, with those who fear You.

How great is the goodness that You have granted me and other Jews, Your Nation. You have given us such great gifts, such precious gifts, that have been stored in Your vast treasuries from the beginning of time, until the coming of the savior and master, Your faithful servant Moses, who brought us Your beloved hidden treasure [the priceless Torah]. All things added together do not equal it. You have done great things, my God, for the Jewish People as a whole and for each and every one of us, every single day.

For all of these may Your Name be praised and elevated and exalted, our King, for ever and ever. We shall praise You and speak of Your wonders — for our lives that are totally in Your hands, for our souls that are entrusted to You, for Your miracles that are with us each and every day, for Your wonders and kindnesses that are present at all times, morning, noon and night. [You] are Good, for Your compassion never ends, and [You] are the Merciful One, Your kindnesses never cease; our hopes are always upon You.

The Holy Land

Now that I have come before You, God, Who always grants undeserved favors, let Your compassion flow over me from Your Treasury of Unearned Gifts, and allow me to ascend to the Land of Israel, quickly and soon, this year. Perhaps there I will merit to gain holiness and sanctity, from the ten levels of holiness that are found in the Holy Land, so that I might from now on be able to return to You sincerely, to sanctify and purify myself henceforth and forever, and to merit true fear of Heaven.

Master of the Universe, I have no mouth with which to speak, no courage with which to lift up my head. I, a sinner, confused and inarticulate, come as a pauper at the door, asking and begging for a gift, in the merit of the great tzaddikim who were worthy of reaching the Holy Land after overcoming many obstacles. They managed through their efforts to extend the Treasury of Unearned Gifts to the entire world.

Solely upon their merit and strength do I rely and come before You, even now, to request and beg from You an allocation from Your Treasury of Unearned Gifts which is available to the tzaddikim; may You grant me in Your vast compassion and great kindness, the ability to do whatever is necessary to enable me to walk in Your path and heed Your mitzvot, from now until eternity.

Grant me merit, show me, teach me the correct path and give me the proper advice that I will soon merit overcoming all the obstacles, hurdles, barriers and confusion that prevent me from going to the Land of Israel. Whether the obstacles are financial or any other kind — in particular if they are emotional or mental blocks — let me be worthy of overcoming them all very, very quickly, so that I may soon arrive safe and sound in the Promised Land.

May I merit there to draw upon myself holiness, sanctity and absolute fear of Heaven, from the ten levels of sanctity that are found in the Holy Land.

For these ten levels of sanctity correspond to the Ten Sayings with which You created Your world, and within these Ten Sayings are contained the Ten Commandments, which include the entire Torah, comprising every type of holy fear.

Master of the Universe, Mighty, Fearsome and Awesome: please enable me to attain all this fear and sanctity, so that I will return to You in true repentance, and serve You honestly out of fear and love: to study, teach, guard and observe all the precepts of Your Torah with love.

Repentance

Master of the Universe, what can I say? You know me. You have already informed us that we must pray a great deal because You listen to the prayers of every mouth. I rely on this as I come before You in prayer, Master of compassion, Master of kindness, Master of mercy. I'm hoping to quickly ascend to the Land of Israel — perhaps there I will merit to find a path, strength, and true advice that I will be able to follow, in order to draw near to You with truth, fear and love, and to honestly and finally return to You.

Father in Heaven, Who always devises plans to prevent those distant from You from being lost: Please don't embarrass me for having hoped [in You], don't disappoint me, don't shut Your ears to my cries, don't harden Your heart against Your son, do not hide Your face from my longing, my yearning, for I have for some time desired to return to You in earnest.

Have compassion on me so that from this point onward You will bring me near to You and to Your service. Don't deal with me according to my sins, according to my deeds. Because You know my evil inclination, You know me — from where I've come, where I've been, from beginning to end. You have the ability to remove from me the wickedness of my heart and my stubbornness; the overwhelming strength of my lusts and the brazenness of my physical tendencies. For everything is in Your hands; in Your hands are strength and might, in Your hands lies the power to elevate and strengthen all.

Therefore, upon You alone have I cast my hopes, upon You I rely, for You are mighty and powerful enough to save me. You can do anything and nothing can be denied You — for who can tell You what to do? "Bring me back [to You] and I will return, for You are my God. Heal me, God, and I will be healed" — in body and in soul. "Save me, and I will be saved; because You are my praise!"

In the merit of the great tzaddikim who are truly humble, who are straightforward and who behave as ordinary people do, grant me [a gift] from Your Treasury of Unearned Gifts. You alone know the great holiness, awesome levels and tremendous strength of these tzaddikim. They can elevate even me and bring me closer to You and to the Holy Land. They can make me worthy of fixing all that I have ruined so that I won't die without having first corrected the damage I've done. So boundless is their merit!

"God! Create for me a pure heart. Renew within me a straightforward spirit. Help me! Return to me the joy of Your salvation. Support me with Your generous love." Help me! Help me! Save me! Save me! For to You alone have I spread my arms in supplication. "I have spread my arms in prayer the entire day, my soul is like parched land, longing for You. From the ends of the earth I cry out to You. When my heart is faint, You lead me to high ground. My soul yearns and pines for the courtyard of God; my heart and my flesh sing out to the Living God. God! You are my Lord and I shall pray to You. My soul thirsts for You, my flesh pines for You, parched and weary, without water, to see Your Sanctuary, to witness Your power and glory."

Simplicity

Let it be Your will, our God and God of our fathers, Who is generous in kindness and in goodness: take pity on me in Your great compassion and teach me and direct me in the ways of genuine simplicity. Let me be innocently artless with You, my God, and let me do Your will straightforwardly, without any futile sophistication.

For You, God, know that there is no way for a person to draw near to You other than through complete, sincere simplicity, with pure faith. And I believe, and even understand to some extent, that even in our deep spiritual descent, in the depths of this bitter exile of body and soul — there are pathways of simplicity and faith through which anyone, under any circumstances, can find vitality and discover a straight and simple path and sound advice, and thus draw close to You.

Even someone who has fallen so very far — anyone — can find paths by which to ascend from his fall and to draw near to You, to cry out to You and to entreat You with simple sincere prayers and with complete faith. For this is Your desire, as is written, "My eyes are upon the faithful of the world that they may dwell with Me; he who goes on a simple path will serve Me." "Fortunate are those whose path is simple, who walk in the way of the Torah of God."

Master of the Universe, Who grants unearned gifts in every generation, in Your compassion and kindness You created and sustained Your world which was unworthy for twenty-six generations [over 2,400 years], until the giving of the Torah. For at that time the world endured, not through the merit of the Torah, but because of the benefits You granted from Your Treasury of Unearned Gifts.

Take pity on us now as well, in Your great compassion. Open up to us Your goodly Treasury, Your Treasury of Unearned Gifts, and act towards us with charity and unearned kindness at all times, even during those times when we are distant from Torah. Have pity on us in the merit of the genuine tzaddikim and bestow upon us all goodness. Sustain us with unearned kindness, as You did for all mankind for twenty-six generations before the giving of the Torah.

Torah study

Master of the Universe, have compassion on us for Your Name's sake. Help us and grant us merit that we may involve ourselves in Your Torah, day and night. Let me study Torah with perseverance, with holiness and purity, for the sake of Your Holy Name. Open up my heart to Your pure and perfect holy Torah, that I may merit to understand and realize its depth, pleasantness and sweetness.

Teach me how to conduct myself in Torah study in every situation: when to study and when to "neglect Torah study for the sake of fulfilling the Torah." Let me be diligent in Torah study day and night, and let me know when is the right time to refrain from studying, so that everything will fit into its proper place in my schedule.

For You, Master of all, Giver of the Torah, know that we are mere flesh and blood, clods of earth, and there are times we cannot study Torah. We need to eat, drink and sleep. We must earn a living and take care of our other physical needs. There are also times when our minds cannot sustain incessant study and we must interrupt our studies so that our minds do not become overwhelmed and confused.

In truth, considering the holiness, sweetness and pleasantness found in the Torah, it would be appropriate for us to study Torah ceaselessly, for "it is our life and the length of our days." How can we ever separate ourselves from true life, even if only for a moment? But You have already revealed to us that it is impossible to avoid separating ourselves from Torah study, for we must take care of our physical needs.

Therefore, take pity on us in Your great compassion, and allow us to draw near to the genuine tzaddikim, who sustain the world with their Torah study, with their holiness and with their wondrous pathways of straightforwardness; in their merit may we draw holiness, vitality and everything good upon ourselves, at all times, from Your Treasury of Unearned Gifts that is available to them. For [when they must be distant from the Torah] it is through this Treasury that they sustain themselves and sustain all the ordinary people in the world: Torah scholars when they must refrain from their studies; common folk; those who, because of their many sins, are buried deep in the mires of the nether worlds; even the gentile nations.

All are sustained through the pathways of the great tzaddikim, who must occasionally act as common folk. Then those tzaddikim draw vitality and bounty from the same source that sustained the world prior to the giving of the Torah, when the world subsisted on unearned gifts, through the Concealed Torah, which is the path which leads to the Holy Land.

Drawing near to the tzaddikim

Please! God, Who is full of compassion. Grant us the merit to draw near and to be always associated with these tzaddikim, who have the power to bring vitality to all mankind even when they are distant from Torah. For You are full of compassion and You know that at this time we have no strength, vitality or existence, except through the strength and merit of these awesome and holy tzaddikim. Help us, grant us merit, that we may draw near to them, fulfill their teachings and walk with sincerity in their pathways, and that we may act simply in a sincere manner and with pure faith, without a "sophisticated," convoluted approach.

Faith

Grant me the merit to sustain myself and to bring joy to my soul through faith alone — for this is the basis of everything. And grant me the knowledge and belief that You created the world with Ten Sayings within which are concealed the Ten Commandments which comprise the entire Torah. All that is found in the world — all business and trading, all thoughts, words and deeds in the world — all is contained in the Ten Sayings through which all was created.

For in these Ten Sayings are concealed the Ten Commandments, which contain and are the outline for the entire Torah. Through this faith may I merit to attach myself to You and to the Torah at all times, at every moment, through true simplicity, even when I must refrain from Torah study.

Never despair!

Strengthen my heart that it never fail, and let not the evil inclination weaken my resolve under any circumstances. Let me always know and believe with pure faith that there is never cause for despair in the world — none whatsoever — no matter what! For Your mercy is never-ending.

You test every person at all times and You cause many awesome events to occur and Your desire is that each person should constantly strengthen himself in You, even if he is very distant from You — for no good desire is ever lost. Each good desire is very precious to You. Each movement that a person makes to draw near to You, from wherever he may be, is extremely precious and dear to You.

You have begun to reveal a modicum of Your extensive, awesome and wondrous compassion through the holy tzaddikim, who have taken us by the hand, strengthened us and proclaimed, "Never despair!"

Avoiding strife

Master of the Universe, Who is filled with compassion, You know that the Jewish Nation is now at the end of its bitter exile, for the time of our redemption is very near. You await, moment by moment, our salvation. The souls of Your People long with unprecedented yearning to serve You.

But the Evil Inclination has extended itself in its efforts, to confuse the entire world, and has brought a tremendous amount of intense strife into the world. Terrible arguments have broken out even among the righteous; many shameless people have claimed leadership. Even amongst the authentic Torah scholars there are bitter arguments, to the point that no one can recognize the truth.

Have compassion on us, for the sake of Your Name. Grant us merit that we shall have no part of any conflict against the righteous. Smile upon us with Your Treasury of Unearned Gifts and reveal to us the real truth, that we may be able to recognize the genuine tzaddikim in our generation, and that we may draw near to them and have a share in their merit, and walk in their pathways with sincerity, simplicity and faith, devoid of any of the empty sophisticated philosophies prevalent in the world today.

May I come to a state of true joy at all times, through simplicity and through complete faith in You and Your Torah and in the genuine tzaddikim. Take pity on me and strengthen my heart so that I long, yearn and desire to travel to the Holy Land. I will pray daily for this merit, until You open up for me the Treasury of Unearned Gifts and grant me an unearned gift and help me to travel to the Holy Land quickly, without mishap, and to draw upon myself the ten levels of sanctity of the Holy Land.

Joy

Father in Heaven! Help me! Save me with Your wondrous ways, with Your wise counsel, according to the dictates of the simplicity of the genuine tzaddikim, so that I will be able to overcome all the spiritual backsliding that I have experienced until now. May "He Who said to His world, 'Enough!' say 'Enough!' to my troubles." Give me at all times wise, wondrous advice that will enable me to rejoice — even with humor or some trivial foolishness if need be — and "God's joy shall be my strength" always, until with Your great mercy and Your gifts You will bear me quickly to the Holy Land. Perhaps there I will merit to draw near to You and to begin anew to serve You sincerely with fear and love, with simplicity, truth and faith, as is Your will.

God! Full of compassion! My King and God to Whom I pray! Hear my prayers, accept my humble supplications, answer my entreaties if I find favor in Your eyes; all that I request is in the merit of the true tzaddikim. Take action for their sake and answer my requests and petitions: be with me and help me from this moment on, so that I may truly turn away from evil and do that which is good in Your eyes. Cause my soul to rejoice always, and allow me to strengthen myself with joy at all times, to make myself happy with all types of permissible joy, even foolishness if necessary, so that I will always be filled with happiness.

Help me achieve pure faith, and enable me to walk in the paths of simplicity, as is Your will, until I "fly" quickly to the Holy Land, and arrive there safely, and merit there all that is truly and eternally good. Let my physical body put no obstacles in my path. Let the true tzaddikim succeed in working with me: with my *nefesh, ruach* and *neshamah* (soul, spirit and higher soul), and with my body, as they wish, not as my physicality would dictate, God forbid. Let me submit my will to Your will and to the will of the true, holy tzaddikim.

The Treasury of Unearned Gifts

Master of the Universe! Master of all! Take pity on me and answer my prayers. Favor me from Your Treasury of Unearned Gifts: Draw me to You with absolute compassion and great mercy. Bring me quickly to the Holy Land as an unearned gift. After all, for whom did You create the Treasury of Unearned Gifts?

The tzaddikim do not need unearned gifts because they are deserving of their rewards through their own merits! And even when they are forced to refrain from Torah study and become like ordinary people, at which time they draw upon the Treasury of Unearned Gifts for their sustenance and vitality — this, too, is a very great act of devotion on their part. From these devotions You receive great pleasure, and for this they deserve immense additional reward. Furthermore, You have informed us through Your genuine tzaddikim that the wicked do not benefit from the Treasury of Unearned Gifts.

It follows that the main purpose of the Treasury of Unearned Gifts is to give satisfaction to those tzaddikim who wish to bring Your backsliding children closer to You. Thus, even when the tzaddikim become like ordinary people, they can draw sustenance from the Treasury of Unearned Gifts in order to enliven and give vitality to all those who have become distant from You. Then the tzaddikim can support, assist and strengthen even those who have fallen and greatly distanced themselves from You. They can receive and pass along sustenance from the Treasury of Unearned Gifts and thus encourage the multitudes to return to You.

Upon this I rely and from afar I look forward with hope to a happy ending. I present myself before You with great audacity, to ask You to bring me speedily to the Holy Land, the Land of Life, the Land of Holiness. Draw me near to You in sincerity, as I have beseeched You, the Compassionate One, according to the dictates of simplicity and absolute faith and in true joy.

"May God finish for me; God! Your lovingkindness is eternal. Do not abandon Your handiwork." "May the words of my mouth and the desires of my heart find favor before You, God." Amen! Amen!

* * *